More Praise for *Birth 2012 and Beyond* and for Barbara Marx Hubbard

"Success in building a sustainable world is impossible without the kind of inspired heart-focused vision that Barbara provides in this important book."
— Alisa Gravitz, executive director of Green America

"Imagine bringing together the world's most conscious innovators into a single campaign of personal and global transformation. What new possibilities might be unleashed? This book by our beloved visionary Barbara Marx Hubbard and her team of transformational leaders shows you how to think way out of the box—exactly what we now need!"
— Chip Conley, founder of Joie de Vivre Hotels and author of *Emotional Equations*

"Barbara Marx Hubbard is a true pioneer of evolutionary spirituality. Long before the rest of us, she awakened to the 'impulse of evolution' and became tangibly transformed by it. Her life is a compelling story of a relentless and passionate commitment to a new conception of what it means to be human in a cosmos that is awakening to itself. *Birth 2012 and Beyond* is a powerful introduction to her life's message and mission."
— Andrew Cohen, founder of EnlightenNext, author of *Evolutionary Enlightenment*

"Barbara Marx Hubbard is one of the crucial pioneers in the movement toward conscious evolution. Her ideas are powerful, transformative, and necessary. This present work continues her mission of awakening and inspiring people to become cocreative partners with Gaia, bringing Buckminster Fuller's design science approach into the twenty-first century."
— Daniel Pinchbeck, founder of Evolver.net

"Barbara Marx Hubbard perfectly explains the new era of humanity that starts on December 22, 2012! This book is sure to be a big hit."

—don Miguel Ruiz, *New York Times* bestselling author of *The Four Agreements*

"*Birth 2012 and Beyond* envisions a future to embrace with love rather than face with fear. It offers individual and collective tools for giving birth to what is most beautiful in ourselves and in the world around us. Barbara Marx Hubbard is our undisputed planetary midwife."

—Marianne Williamson, *New York Times* #1 bestselling author

"When I saw our precious planet from space, I recognized that we must shift our consciousness and culture before we destroy our fragile home. This inspired and visionary book offers profound wisdom for how to make the shift in time."

—Edgar Mitchell, Apollo 14 astronaut, founder of Institute of Noetic Sciences

"There is no doubt in my mind that Barbara Marx Hubbard—who helped introduce the concept of futurism to society—is the best informed human now alive regarding futurism and the foresights it has produced."

—Buckminster Fuller

"Barbara is a true visionary, demonstrating by her words and actions her commitment to a sustainable future."

—John Denver

"Renowned as a futurist, Barbara Marx Hubbard also plants her feet firmly in today."

—Gene Roddenberry

Birth 2012
and Beyond

Birth 2012 and Beyond

Humanity's Great Shift to the
Age of Conscious Evolution

Barbara Marx Hubbard
with the Welcoming Committee

Shift Books

www.shiftmovement.com

Copyright © 2012
By Barbara Marx Hubbard

Cover design by Stevee Postman
Interior design by Diane Rigoli

Library of Congress Control Number: 2011943613

ISBN: 978-0-9848407-0-0

    Hubbard, Barbara Marx, 1929-
        Birth 2012 and beyond : humanity's great shift to the age of conscious evolution / Barbara Marx Hubbard; with the Welcoming Committee.
        p. cm.
        Includes bibliographical references.
        LCCN 2011943613
        ISBN 978-0-9848407-0-0

    1. Social evolution. 2. Social ethics. 3. Social participation.   I. Title.

HM626.H825 2012   303.4
                   QBI12-600027

First printing March 2012
Printed in the United States of America on recycled paper. ♻

10 9 8 7 6 5 4 3 2

Contents

Part III: Welcoming the Birth

Part IV: Resources for the Birth

Recommended Resources

Recommended Reading

Affiliated Organizations

Special Essays

Foreword:
Birthing a New Era

By Stephen Dinan, CEO and founder, The Shift Network

Every so often, humanity's evolution accelerates to the point that it becomes visible to all: think of the early spread of Buddhism, the flowering of democracy in ancient Athens, the Renaissance, the Scientific Revolution, the Reformation, the founding of the American republic—and more recently, the Civil Rights Movement and the Arab Spring, to name a few.

At the heart of these times of accelerated change are astounding geniuses and inspired pioneers. We love to celebrate these icons, but the flowering of a new era of human possibility never rests upon the work of a single individual.

Individual leadership is crucial, but real change flows from a collective wave of new consciousness that is networked and interconnected—a vast interweaving of simmering passions, fresh ideas, new memes, and bold visions that emerge when the time is truly right. As such an evolutionary wave grows, the pioneers encourage each other to go beyond what they've inherited from preceding generations. They experiment with new ways of being, new ways of seeing, new possibilities for living. They seek patterns that express more of our full human potential—politically, socially, and artistically.

Sometimes, of course, things gets messy. If leaders of a particular emergence are met with resistance from the status quo, the urgency in the push toward the new can result in impatience, stridence, and even violence. Yet at the core is love: love for humanity, love for what we may still become, love for justice and freedom, love for the creative process of evolution itself.

The birthing of a new consciousness whose time has truly come cannot be halted, in the same sense that the gestation and delivery of a baby cannot be reversed; its birth is a *one-way journey*. Similarly, the birth of a new era may face titanic challenges and, often, apparent defeats. But the end result is the arrival of something fundamentally new.

At such moments in history, the true potency and glory of the human race shines through. We are revealed as creatures with enormous capacity for goodness, creativity, and generosity. We are able to remember, once again, that we can forge a better society, one that shines with beauty, radiates truth, and encourages us toward a barely intuited future.

We are at such a crucial point of evolution right now, but this time it's on an unprecedented planetary scale. Previous evolutions have taken place in a single culture and only gradually spread their influence. But today, with 24/7 media and the Internet, our global heart increasingly now beats as one. Protests can spread immediately through news feeds, Facebook, and Twitter; ideas and visions can propagate at the speed of light. We easily travel and intermingle with each other both physically and in our minds. Our consciousness has become global in a way that humanity has never before experienced. As Barbara Marx Hubbard would put it, the noosphere is getting its collective eyes. And this new reality of instant global communication opens the door for the possibility of a global renaissance—a great Birth of a new era of human culture.

This Birth is inevitable in some ways, since—as Barbara Marx Hubbard makes clear throughout this book—the impulse towards evolution, freedom, and higher possibility runs deeply in each of us. We all want an expanded life, a wider heart, more wholeness, a freer future. And, once we taste it, we do not easily relinquish the dream.

We can, of course, slide back for a time—regressing into old fears and habits, squandering our opportunities through infighting, demonization, and war.

But such a regression is something we cannot afford now. We've simply grown too powerful with weapons of mass destruction, too numerous with a population of seven billion citizens, and too impactful with the dramatic rise of global mass consumerism. Backsliding is far more costly now than it's ever been. The systems of life maintenance on which we now depend as a species sit at a critical crossroads; we must turn immediately toward their restoration or face irreversible decline.

Going back, then, is not a viable option. We must go forward into the Birth of a new humanity that Barbara has spent decades telling us about, or we don't go forward at all. Our only real choice is between whether to do so gracefully, with wisdom, passion, and a good dose of celebration, or dragging our heels, increasing the pain of the transition.

The truth is that humanity *is* on the precipice of a new era of peace, sustainability, health, and prosperity— that is, *if* enough of us dare to declare it and shed the beliefs and behaviors that have governed us for millennia. We have the opportunity now to bring to fruition the longest-held dreams of our world: the end of war, democracy for all, eradication of hunger, and education for everyone. Freedom. Opportunity. Global friendship.

These dreams are at our fingertips now, so close that we can almost touch them and envision them coming to pass in our lifetimes. Despite appearances, it is a time for rejoicing!

And so, my questions for you are:

Why not make *this* year of 2012 (and the years to come) the defining moment in human history during which we turn things around?

What if we come together at an unprecedented scale to cleanse ourselves of violence, commit ourselves to health, pledge ourselves to generosity, and state our intentions for a new kind of world where we are all respectful, loving members of a single human family living in harmony with all creation?

What if we harness the power of media and the Internet to commit to these things in ways that are powerful, fun, engaging, and life-changing?

Why not create a "planetary gestation" that culminates with hundreds of millions celebrating the Birth of this new era on the suitably auspicious date of December 22, 2012— "Day One" for a new epoch of human possibility?

And, what if we were to renew these commitments every year after on that day, until the dream becomes a reality?

What if we *can* do this together—making the Birth irresistible to all our brothers and sisters without exception?

If we could stand together for the Birth, not only would that be a great service to our world, but it would be a great blessing to each of us who has witnessed, in horror, sadness, and grief the devastation that has preceded us. What a birthday present to the world and to ourselves to leave that era behind and enter a new one, resplendent with joyous opportunity and infinite possibility.

I suspect you have this book in your hands because you are part of that service to humanity—you are an integral part of the Birth. And I believe you know, deep in your soul, that it is time to proclaim the new era. *This* is the moment to call forth the hundreds of millions of souls who also recognize that now is the time for the discord to cease, people who are ready, like you, to declare an end to the disharmony, and commit to an age of peace and cocreativity.

If you are called in this manner, we ask you to collaborate with us. We need you to collaborate with us. And by "us," I mean a growing global movement of people who are willing to serve this Great Shift together and make 2012, and beyond, the time for declaring the Birth of a new world. We will celebrate this global renaissance with an unprecedented event befitting the momentous occasion of a planetary convergence—and commit to implementing this vision in the years ahead.

On this journey, we are blessed by extraordinary guides, a few of whom are showcased in this book, and thousands of whom I've been privileged to meet through The Shift Network that we began just two years ago.

First, of course, is Barbara Marx Hubbard herself, who has stepped forward as our prophetic voice for the Birth, offering us motherly blessing, wisdom, and encouragement as we make it through the tumult of the planetary birth canal. She has been coded with a deep knowing of how the Birth unfolds, helping each of us to remember our best role in the unfolding. She blesses us with a mother's unconditional love, a philosopher's wide-ranging intellect, and a visionary's soaring spirit. Barbara offers us not only a new template for human evolution but a new template for the planetary elder as well, showing us that at 82 years of age, one's greatest gifts are ageless. After presenting her full vision for the Birth in Part I of this book, Barbara explains in detail in Part II important ways in which you can participate now and into the future.

Standing with her in calling forth this global Birth are members of what we call "the Welcoming Committee"—

a circle of twelve leaders, teachers, and pioneers, beacons of light who offer their wisdom, blessing, and passionate work in the service of this collective shift. In Part III of this book, each shares their insights for how we can navigate this time in such a way that it leads to something unprecedented. They are welcoming us into a new era, and celebrating the emergence of the "baby" into a new world. As a council, they model the synergy that is at the core of the new era: the commitment to move beyond competition to heartfelt and even divinely inspired collaboration.

In the coming pages, we explore the context for the Birth and how it lives in each of us. We describe how you can get involved in the Shift, and outline how we envision the nine months from Conception Day (March 22, 2012) to the Planetary Birth Day (December 22, 2012) unfolding, as well as what is to come after our new planet is symbolically born. We don't expect to get all the details perfect (or even vaguely correct). What we will do is lay out a template for how we can make the celebration of our Planetary Birth the most positive evolutionary event the world has ever seen. Whether that vision (or another that is still more refined) becomes reality, is really up to each of us.

The years behind us have prepared us for systemic change, with economic meltdowns, political gridlock, environmental destruction, unrest, and fear. The breakdowns of the old systems have become painfully evident; *Time* magazine chose "the protestor" as the Person of the Year for 2011 to reflect the global uprising of discontent aimed at moneyed elites, oppressive dictators, unaccountable corporations, and aloof politicians.

These developments have provided what Barbara likes to call the "contractions" that signal the Birth of the new. We have recognized that the old systems are not serving us anymore and, more importantly, that the old consciousness is no longer working either. We've reached the end game for greed. And the heartache we feel when we witness a world of poverty, hunger, and deprivation can itself spark the flowering of viable innovations and compassionate solutions. (Barbara calls the threats that spur us toward solutions "evolutionary drivers".)

Evolution has led us to understand that a world built on love is our antidote to fear and selfishness; a world infused with community is our antidote to isolation; a world colored with beauty and justice is our antidote to the hard boot of oppression. Let us each stand for that world in our unique brilliance and creativity. Let us each dare to be midwives and "mid-husbands" for the Birth. Let us each declare our world as sacred, worthy of our most sincere service.

The pages you are now reading are only a beginning. The rest of the story is yours to cocreate. In the broadest sense, you are truly an author of this text, because it is not something that you simply receive. This is an invitation to join us as a cocreator, sharing your magic, telling your tale, offering your Gift to the Shift on planet Earth.

It promises to be a grand adventure! Let us begin with Barbara, our prophetic guide.

Appreciation

Birth 2012 and Beyond is a very small book with a huge purpose for humankind: to bring to millions of people a far greater awareness of the potential of our Planetary Birth and our emergence as a universal species. Yet, how does one even begin to offer in a simple and inviting way such an enlarged understanding of our future? As I pondered this question, I was blessed with the participation of two extraordinary evolutionary women, my friends and cocreators in writing this book: Jan Phillips, writer, artist, and advocate of evolutionary creativity; and Judy Cauley, my thought partner, educational leader, and member of the Congregation of St. Joseph.

Jan Phillips engaged me in the dialogues that are at the heart of Part I of this book. Judy Cauley worked closely with me to bring this conversation into its final form. The three of us became a cocreative evolutionary circle—enacting in our editorial process just what we are suggesting is the optimal way to create the Great Planetary Shift. I thank them both with all my heart for this experience of cocreativity in real time. I look forward to our continuing friendship and participation in Birth 2012 and the years beyond.

Of course, my enduring gratitude and love goes to my partner Stephen Dinan, CEO of The Shift Network, who has agreed to produce Birth 2012, and who asked me to do this book so that we could reach millions with the invitation to participate in the Great Shift toward conscious evolution. Thank you, Stephen.

And thanks to Byron Belitsos, the publisher of Shift Books and the chief editor of this book, who has given so much of his loving attention to how we bring this out into the world.

Thanks to Jill Mangino, our publicist, who is giving us the chance to reach more of you with this wonderful invitation to participate in the Birth 2012 Campaign.

I also want to thank Victoria and Ron Friedman of the Vistar Foundation for offering the Vistar Circle method for evolutionary shift circles and their gracious willingness to train, support, and connect these circles worldwide.

Thanks to Claudia Welss, board member of the Foundation for Conscious Evolution and a director of the NextNow Collaboratory as well as the Global Coherence Initiative of the Institute of HeartMath. Claudia brings to this work her vital knowledge of global coherence and subtle energies toward our shared purpose of mass resonance and heart connections, which is so vital to the Planetary Birthing Process.

And, of course, thanks to The Shift Network and to Patricia Gaul, executive director of the Foundation for Conscious Evolution, for all their support in reaching thousands of students with my various teleseminars including Agents of Conscious Evolution, The Emergence Process, and The ACE Guides and Mentors Course, as well as for their ongoing role as catalysts for the Birth 2012 events and beyond.

And finally, but by no means least, gratitude to our blessed Welcoming Committee, whose names and essay titles are listed in our Table of Contents. The essays of these twelve evolutionary pioneers and global cocreators are included in Part III. Through their great work and outreach to over a billion people, these men and women are now leading the way in welcoming humanity toward the next stage of our evolution.

A QR code is like a barcode, and can be scanned by a smart phone's camera.

Note to the Reader:
Using the QR Codes to Access Video

QR codes hail from Japan where they are used quite liberally. A QR code is like a barcode, and can be scanned by a smart phone's camera. You are then directed to a website or other useful information.

What you need in order to scan a QR code:

1. A Smart Phone with a camera

2. An app that reads QR codes. Here are a few:

   • NeoReader (iPhone)

   • ScanLife (Blackberry)

   • Quick Mark (Android)

3. A crisp QR code—we've got them in this book, and also on the back jacket!

The QR codes that we provide direct you to videos of Barbara that supplement the section you are reading. You'll be directed to the URL for the video. **Alternately, you may simply go to this link to find Barbara's videos in sequence: http://tinyurl.com/7dtvmwm.**

Part 1

ENVISIONING
THE BIRTH

 *Chapter 1*

Letter of Invitation to Birth 2012

From Barbara Marx Hubbard

Dear Friends, Colleagues, and Cocreators of the emerging world: Welcome to Birth 2012 and the Birth 2012 Campaign!

This invitation to participate in the Birth is the most important letter I have ever written. Its intent, and the purpose of this book, is to present you with the greatest opportunity that humanity has ever consciously faced together: the effort to cocreate a planetary shift in time to avert global catastrophe by helping humanity cross the gap from "Here"—our current breakdowns—to "There"—our future of infinite possibility.

Why is this invitation so urgent?

Because our current condition of over-growth in our finite Earth system is simply not sustainable.

We will either evolve toward a more sustainable, compassionate, and creative global system, or we face the real possibility of devolution and destruction of our life support system and of much of life on Earth—within our own or our children's lifetime!

This dangerous reality is motivating us to enter into what I call *the first age of conscious evolution*—that is, evolution by choice and not by chance. It means that we need to be *causal* in the actions and direction we take in *this* lifetime. What is being required of us is to learn to co-evolve with nature and cocreate with Spirit.

Again, why do I say that the timing is so urgent? Why now? Can't we wait a while and see how it turns out? No, we can't wait. It's like the birth of a baby. You might not be ready, but if the baby is ready, it's coming out *now* for better or for worse. It can either be a disastrous birth, or a gentle one.

We are being called to a great experiment, for no one alive on Earth knows how to make such a vast evolutionary shift in this short of a time. For the first time in our conscious history we are being given the opportunity to guide and ease our transition to the next stage of evolution. This situation is new for humanity, for we are the first Earth species to consciously face evolution or extinction.

This condition may be new for us, but it is *not* novel for the universe. Evolution operates by "punctuated equilibrium," meaning long periods of slow change that are punctuated by apparent sudden jumps. For billions of years, nature has been going through such creative leaps. It has progressed from energy evolving into matter, to planets like our Earth, to primitive life, to animal life, to human life, and now to us going around the next turn on the Spiral of Evolution toward the next phase of humanity. When we review this Big History, this deep-time past, we learn that certain lessons recur:

Crises almost always precede transformation.

Problems are evolutionary drivers.

Nature takes jumps through greater synergy and cooperation within and among species.

We are facing transformative crises and living through such a leap now—the great wake-up call for the maturation of humanity.

We have reached what systems theorists call a "chaos point." When a system in chaos is far from equilibrium, it tries to right itself by going backward to the old; this is why we see reactive movements everywhere in society right now. But an evolving system cannot return to the past. It must seek out new structures and systems, and quickly ascend to a new configuration—or else face rapid decline. Fortunately, according to the theory, small positive fluctuations in this sea of social chaos can jump the system to such a higher order.

This book is dedicated to the fact that *we* can each be that small fluctuation! The opportunity now being offered to us from the sacred process of evolution is to participate in creating many positive fluctuations as pioneering souls. We are being called upon to shift from ego-centrism to living from our Essential Selves; to discover our vocations of destiny; to give our unique Gift to the Shift; to work toward maximum global coherence; and to evolve our communities, our world, and ourselves.

In other words, our opportunity, right now, is to become planetary birthing mamas and papas! Joining together, we can "gentle the birth" of a Universal Humanity connected through the heart to the whole of life—and guide our Earth community into its next evolutionary stage.

I am deeply grateful to have lived long enough to see this awakening actually happening for millions of us now. I am additionally grateful to be joined in this book by our brilliant, inaugural Welcoming Committee of evolutionary pioneers, each giving us their message, and indeed their lives, to foster our emergence now.

As Stephen Dinan reminds us in both the Foreword and the Afterword, December 21, 2012, has been identified by Mayan prophecy as the end of a long cosmic cycle. Therefore, Dec 22, 2012, has been selected by me and Stephen to be our planetary "due date," the new *Day One* for the next era of evolution.

As you will discover in this book, a profound awareness of an impending planetary shift came to me in 1966 as a deep personal revelation, when I knew nothing about the Mayan calendar or other prophecies. This event was a flash of expanded reality that I call the Planetary Birth Experience. At that moment my inner knowing understood these words in my heart: *Our crisis is a birth*. I saw that what all the great avatars and mystics of humanity have told us is true: We are one; we are whole; we are good; and we are being born as a Universal Humanity within a universe of immeasurable intelligence, energy, and dimension. In this vision, I was shown that we are a product of universal evolution, from the flaring forth after the Big Bang to the historical present, and I was guided to *go tell the story of our birth*. The amazing part now is that everything I experienced in that epiphany so many years ago is now happening in real time.

I have discovered in the last forty-six years of communicating our evolutionary potential that this newly understood Universe Story is actually imprinted in our hearts, our bodies, and in our souls. The universe is unfolding and manifesting in us. We *are* the universe in person! Each of us is the composite expression of the 13.7 billion years of evolution, no matter what our culture, age, faith, or worldview.

When we work together for the great superordinate goal of cocreating a planetary shift, we awaken this ever-expanding creativity and potentiality within ourselves. The lid comes off our life purpose, and our "inner Big Bang" turns on! *We* are flaring forth.

When anyone says "Yes! I want to give my Gift to the Shift. Yes! I want to help gentle humanity's birth," this "yes" mobilizes spirit-in-action within each of us and opens us to the Impulse of Evolution. And it is for this reason that this work leads us to experience such a deep and intrinsic personal fulfillment.

Intention creates and the universe is responsive to requests. It's waiting for us to wake up and connect with each other. In other words, the universe is urging us to cooperate with the process of creation in alignment with nature's tendency to evolve to higher consciousness, greater freedom, and more complex and synergistic order. It calls us to be receptive to what is within us and beyond us and to move together toward a cocreative society in which each person is free to be and do their best. When we activate this inner process of Creation *together* throughout the world, miracles occur.

That's why I invite you to join us and millions of people around the world in co-evolving a new Earth and a new Humanity. I look forward with joy to our shared participation and our collective revelation as we discover together the mystery at work in Birth 2012 and beyond. Yours in love and faith in our potential to evolve,

Barbara Marx Hubbard
January 25, 2012
Santa Barbara, California

View Barbara's personal invitation to the
Birth 2012 Campaign.

Chapter 2

My Vision of the
Planetary Birth

Many of my best ideas have arisen in the resonant field that results when I enter into deep dialogue with trusted friends and colleagues. My extended conversation with Jan Phillips that took place over a four-day period in November, 2011, is a perfect example. We have edited the dialogue which is presented in the next two chapters.

This first chapter traces my own personal evolution over many years that has inexorably led to our Birth 2012 Campaign.

Many people are dwelling on the prophecies related to the Mayan calendar, which as you know simply stops on December 21, 2012, and they are wondering what that means for the planet. You've suggested that 2012 could mark, symbolically, the advent of a sustainable planetary civilization and of a new species of humankind. And, long ago you reframed our global crises as "a crisis of birth." Can you amplify on these intriguing ideas?

Well, we all understand the meaning of biological birth—it's the most amazing thing. From a little fertilized egg comes this remarkable mystery: the gradual transformation from a zygote to a fetus to an infant. But eventually the new being begins to overgrow the womb, to kick and move. It then enters a dangerous, final phase of crisis. The new baby is preparing to move through the birth canal into the world. And, as soon as it's born, it is cut off from its mother's resources. It panics—it's taking its first breath! Birth is clearly a dangerous moment in the life of a biological organism.

Humankind is having a comparable birthing experience on a macro scale. If you look at planet Earth as a whole system, it's obvious that we're overpopulating, we're polluting, and we're running out of resources. Like an infant that is reaching the "due date" of its birth, we're overgrowing "the womb" of the Earth. Our "birthing" crisis is inflicting pain and suffering for millions, as well as the possible destruction of our life support system.

The urgency of our global crisis is causing people to wake up all over the planet. It's dawning on us that something creative—something new—is pressing within us to emerge. What is now being born is transforming the old situation with the prospect of new solutions; and, at the same time, it is helping to create a new world—a world that we have in some respect always held in our hearts. It's offering a better future, a more equitable future, a more peaceful future, a more evolving future, a future that has been mystically realized by great visionaries as something that transcends our current condition.

And so, I believe the following intuition is accurate: our crisis is *potentially* the birth of a more co-evolving, cocreative humanity.

Can you define for us what you mean by "cocreative humanity"?

By "cocreative" I mean the ability to access what I call the "Impulse of Evolution." The impulse in this case refers to the process of creation and evolution that has moved life for billions of years toward greater consciousness and complexity. That impulse is *in* each of us. As it turns on, we start evolving and we want to express more of our potential. Further, it seems to me that, animated as we are by this impulse to evolve, a new type of human is emerging in the face of our shared global crisis. I call these pioneers "universal humans," because they are connected through the heart to the whole of life. They are awakening from within with a desire to find greater life purpose, and are lit up with a mysterious sense of the future. This new person is moving toward cosmic consciousness and an ever-deepening spirituality.

Just as this cocreative human is emerging, we also notice that numerous paradigm-shifting innovations in every field are arising: in health, education, personal and spiritual growth, business, new energy systems, and in more participatory social systems. When we connect these positive innovations with one another, we realize that a new world is already emerging in our midst. Like a newborn infant, something is being born through us that we have never seen before.

My Planetary Birth Epiphany in 1966

That's quite an amazing image. The last great birth story that caused an eruption in global consciousness was the birth of Jesus. I'm wondering if this new birthing story carries the same potential to ignite the public imagination. Do you sense some kind of "mytho-poetic" kinship between this planetary birth story and the birth of Jesus?

Yes, I do. I came to see this important relationship later, but only after a search that took place over many years.

When the United States dropped the atomic bombs on Japan in 1945, I was fifteen years old. After that terrible shock, several great questions arose within me that changed my life. Even today, I believe that our answers to these questions still hold the clues to what is emerging now:

- *What is the meaning of our new power that is good?*

- *What are images of a positive future equal to this power that could attract us?*

While still a teenager, I thought somebody must know where the human race is going that is good—some sort of hopeful vision of a positive future. So, I read widely in world philosophy and religions, looking for that one thing: images and ideas of the positive future equal to our new technological powers. I reasoned that these powers could destroy the world, but they could also evolve it. I saw that. But how? In what direction? I sought a real-world solution, not something available only in life after death or in some metaphysical realm.

A few years later, I had the opportunity to visit President Eisenhower, who was a friend of my father's. It was 1952, just after he'd been elected.

When I was taken into the Oval Office, Eisenhower greeted me. "Hello, young lady." he said. "What can I do for you?"

"Mr. President," I said, "I have a question for you . . . What do you think is the meaning of all our new powers in science and technology that's good? Where are we going?"

He looked startled and shook his head, saying, "I have no idea." It occurred to me then and there that we had better find out!

I continued my research for many years, reading through various philosophies and religions, looking for images of a positive future that could attract us. There was only one text I had read that seemed to give us a vision of where we are going that is good. It was the New Testament.

I had come from a Jewish agnostic family—and had grown up with no religion. My father didn't even tell us we were Jewish! He did not want us to look back toward the old world, only forward toward a new world. Once I asked him, "What religion are we?" He replied, "You're an American, do your best!" As a child, I had wondered what that meant, since I had no sense of direction for myself or for the world.

At one point, in the course of leafing through the New Testament and looking for positive images of the future, I discovered an awesome passage from St. Paul in 1 Corinthians 15: "Behold, I show you a mystery. We shall not all sleep, but we shall all be changed. In a moment, in the twinkling of an eye, at the last trumpet: for the trumpet shall sound and all shall be changed . . . the corruptible shall have put on incorruption. "

I also saw in the writings of John the evangelist that Jesus had said: "Love ye one another . . . You will do what I have been doing and even greater works than these . . ."

There! This resonated in my soul as deeply true. The words of Jesus felt familiar, as though he were a member of my family, someone I had known forever. The scripture profoundly touched my heart. 'Well,' I thought, 'I'll join the church!'

I went down to the local Episcopal Church in Scarsdale, New York. I made an appointment with the minister to ask him my questions: "Is any of this true? How shall we all be changed? How can I be changed?"

There was a pause. I saw immediately, looking into his eyes, that *he didn't know.*

He only said, "Young lady, you go to Sunday School." I did, and to make a long story short, my hopes were not fulfilled.

Many years later, in 1966, I was reading Reinhold Niebuhr, a Christian philosopher and theologian, on the subject of community. He was quoting St. Paul: "For as the body is one, and hath many members, and all the members of that one body, being many, are one body, so also is Christ." Later that day I took a walk behind my home with those words ringing in my ears. It was a freezing winter day in Lakeville, Connecticut. As I contemplated that idea, I felt a deep frustration. The early Christians had a story to tell—no one knows the exact details of Jesus' nativity—but it was one simple story that changed the world: *that a child was born*. Everyone from kings to peasants could understand this story. Suddenly a new question burst forth in my mind. I spoke it out loud, raising my eyes to the icy white sky: "What is *our* story? What in *our* age is a story comparable to the story of the birth of Christ?" I stopped my walk and listened with a poised mind. And the universe responded to me.

The universe responded to you? How did that happen? What was your experience?

I refer to it as an "expanded reality experience." My mind's eye suddenly was in outer space like an astronaut, while at the same time I was aware of myself as a member of the planet. I felt the Earth struggling to coordinate while the mass media was communicating pain through the nervous system of the planet. Our Earth felt like a living organism. It was running out of nonrenewable energy and being polluted, and was torn apart by our overgrowth in the womb of Earth. I felt the pain and suffering of hunger, wars, prisons, the destruction of other species and nature, just as if it were happening in my own body. I felt the whole Earth as one organic whole of which all of us are living members.

The movie of creation that was being presented to me kept unfolding. I then was able to see a few frames ahead into the future. In some mysterious way, it was a forecast of the story of our "birth" on the planetary scale. Empathy started to spread throughout the whole planet. The pain of one was being felt by all. We were connecting with each other, feeling with each other as members of one body.

As empathy increased, spirituality started to emerge from within us. This was not God coming from above or outside us telling us what to do or be. Instead, it was the Spirit within, rising up in each person like a great tide of love, inspiration, and oneness with the source of our being, activating us by the millions. I felt the great light that the mystics speak of radiating outward from within us all.

Then, in a flash, I felt all people on Earth, and the earth itself, being healed, spontaneously. We felt alive, excited, loving one another, filled with expectancy and anticipation. And along with all this, the mass media began to pick up stories of people loving each other, of people being healed, people being creative. The media itself, our global nervous system, was being transformed as it communicated the real *good news* of our breakthroughs.

In that flashing movie-like experience, I saw that when enough of us are connected, there would be a shared feeling of joy and global coherence. In that moment of revelation, I felt waves of unconditional love for the whole planetary body and all Earth-life spreading through millions of us.

Then, something entirely different was yet again presented. I was somehow quickly taken back to the creation of the universe, to the great flaring forth. Out of "no thing at all" came forth "everything that was, is, and will be." It was like a great flash of light unfolding in a brief second that then provided a sped-up movie of creation—like the time-lapse films of a plant from the bulb to the stalk and then to the sudden, unexpected bloom of the flower. I tumbled through the whole 13.7 billion years of evolution, from the formation of energy, matter,

Earth, primitive life, animal life, human life, to us going around the next turn on the spiral of evolution.

The universe had indeed responded to my question. Finally, the vision ended when, deep in my heart, I heard these words: '**Our story is a birth**. It is the birth of humankind as one body. What Christ and all the great avatars came to Earth to tell us is true. We are one, we are good, we are whole, we are being born . . . Go tell the story of our birth, Barbara!'

To see a video interpretation of Barbara's 1966 Birth vision, please use this QR code to view the opening minutes of her DVD, "Visions of a Universal Humanity."

So, after this amazing experience, I can imagine that you were inspired to go out and share the story of our birth. How did you go about telling it at first?

I was completely galvanized and excited by this experience. I ran home and told my husband and five children what had happened. I told them that I felt called to go forth and tell the story of the birth of ourselves as a universal humanity. As you might imagine, they were shocked by my sudden announcement of a new life mission, and they feared that I might even abandon them.

Later, while putting his small arms around me, my nine-year-old son Wade said, "Mom, you are doing what mothers should do. You are creating a future for your children. I know you love us."

I kissed him, holding him in my arms. I told him, "Darling Wade, I love you so much. Your mother's a pioneer and I want you all to come with me . . . let's be pioneers together."

The story of how I went forward from there is told in my autobiography, *The Hunger of Eve*, in my other books, and in *The Mother of Invention* by Neale Donald Walsch.

The Chaos Point: My Birth Vision Forty Years Later

Barbara, here we are all these years after your 1966 vision. Have you found much confirmation for your vision of a planetary birth?

Well, almost everything I had seen in my peak experience is happening now. As we enter the period of 2012 and beyond, a growing awareness of our global crises is intensifying, especially with respect to climate change and the possible destruction of our whole life support system. We are in what philosopher and Welcoming Committee member Ervin Laszlo calls a "chaos point."

Laszlo states, "A chaos point is the crucial tipping point in the evolution of a system in which trends that have brought the system to its present state break down and it can no longer return to its prior states and modes of behavior. It is launched irreversibly on a new trajectory that leads either to breakdown or to breakthrough to a new structure and a new mode of operation." (*The Chaos Point: 2012 and Beyond*, p. vii). In his essay later in this book, "Global Bifurcation: The 2012 Decision Window," Ervin presents our choice in stark terms.

What I have also discovered since 1966 is that we cannot right the current situation by restoring or reforming old forms and structures, including governmental and religious institutions. As I pointed out earlier, they simply can't handle the crises we are facing which, in many ways, they are still causing. We must seek new forms, new structures, and new ways of living that are vital, sustainable, and just—for all Earth life.

Fortunately, these new forms and structures are now emerging. Young "universal humans" are waking up. They are connecting and communicating at the speed of light through cell phones, Twitter, Facebook, and other forms of social networking. Systems theory shows us that small islands of coherence in a sea of chaos can jump a whole system to a higher order. This kind of quantum leap in society is a real possibility now.

Who exactly is part of that small fluctuation? Where in particular are these innovators and leaders located?

It's everyone, everywhere on Earth who is waking up to greater love, purpose, compassion, connectivity, and the desire to cooperate— all those *cultural cocreatives* throughout the world who are committed to a better future. It also includes all believers in any faith tradition on the planet who are able to go beyond the limits of their beliefs and see what resonates as true in their hearts.

What's emerging is far more than a new religion, political party, or enterprise. I believe it's an evolutionary breakthrough of consciousness and creativity with as great a potential as the sudden appearance of self-aware humans fifty thousand years ago. So, are we approaching a planetary birth in real time? It *could* happen when enough people on Earth feel interconnected and coherent as members of one planetary body. This book is a special call to these pioneering souls.

What I do believe is this: We have the resources, technologies, and know-how right now to make the world work for everyone. In fact, we may be just one small fraction of an evolutionary second away from this experience of our "birth" as a universal humanity. But do we have the will and the courage to make it happen?

Cutting through Depression— Getting to Coherence

What an incredible vision! Wouldn't you like to see that in New York Times? *You use the word "coherence" here, and I'm wondering if you could explain that concept a bit more. What kind of coherence do we need to be establishing? Is it a prerequisite for the evolution you are speaking about?*

Coherence is a heartfelt connection with others as part of yourself. What we need now is *global coherence*, an awakening of the global heart, the feeling of being one interconnected planetary body with a shared purpose of mutual growth for the sake of the whole Earth community. My sense is that global coherence is beginning to happen. More and more of us are feeling a heart connection. This means that the Birth may actually be imminent. We will learn much more about "global heart coherence," a concept pioneered by the Institute for HeartMath, later in the book.

Ok, let's say I want to be one of those people. I want to evolve myself to a higher level so I can contribute to the Birth. What is the requirement for being able to add to coherence in this way? For example, if I wanted to have coherence with a person I met on the street, how do I do it? Is it a matter of developing a more compassionate, awakened consciousness?

To begin with, it's that spark of light inside yourself that wants to shine more, that wants to realize its potential, that wants *you* to be a light unto the world. And when you sense that light inside you, your essence literally begins radiating out of you, wanting to connect, contribute, and extend love. When that light turns on inside of you, people can see it in your face. You smile, you willingly give of yourself, and people want to be around you. Even walking down the street or talking in the grocery line—the way you look at a person, the way you open up to them, can make that person feel seen and more alive. So, waking up begins with a feeling of resonance and a sense of intimacy with others. It happens when you no longer see people as "other."

Evolving to a loving place like that is no small challenge. How do we prepare ourselves to do that?

I can tell you what happened to me, and that might point the way to a path for others. As I indicated earlier, it started out with these deep questions: What is the meaning of our power that is good? What are positive images of the future? What is my unique personal gift and how can I give it?

In response, I noticed that an inner creativity was welling up in me. I felt a deep internal pressure that I just couldn't ignore. When this happens, you get an urge to know something, to express something. You start to research it. You don't just sit there. You read books, you reach out, you meet people. And sometimes it doesn't feel like it's working—you get depressed. You don't think you can do it.

In fact, one of the biggest lessons for me was learning the meaning of depression. Only gradually did I realize that depression means that something more wants to be expressed. Before I found my life purpose, I felt depressed and isolated as a housewife even though I loved my children and my husband; I was not in touch with my deeper life purpose, my vocation, my inner creativity. So when I felt depressed, it would have been very easy for me to say, "Struggling for something more is just not worth it."

I needed a sign that something more was possible for me. It was then in the late fifties that I was fortunate to read a book by Betty Friedan called *The Feminine Mystique*. She was one of the "meme-makers" that changed my life. Memes are ideas that build cultures just as genes build bodies, and more will be said about them later in the book. In her book, Betty Friedan interviewed hundreds of women who had been to college, were married, were having many children, and were depressed. She discovered they had a problem without a name. They almost all felt that they had no identity other than wife and mother.

When I read that book, I realized that I was depressed because I had accepted the role of wife and mother as my exclusive identity. In the culture of the 1950s this was the norm; a woman was to get married, have children, take care of her house, take care of her husband. Once I read Betty Friedan, I was encouraged by one major thought: I knew I wasn't alone. And I wasn't willing to accept this depression as normal for me. The meme of *the feminine mystique* liberated and encouraged me to keep seeking.

As I reflected on the American dream of "life, liberty, and the pursuit of happiness," I wondered: *What* is happiness and *who is* actually happy? I felt a subtle mildew growing over the lives of many women including myself. I felt guilty for not being happy. So much was given to me, yet there was this feeling of depression caused by a loss of identity—a deep longing for something more.

So, during this period you realized "the personal was political," so to speak. A societal phenomenon was occurring, and you were entrapped by it. What at first felt like depression later morphed into a higher awareness that something inside you was pressing outward, seeking a release through you. You knew you were here to express something creative, but the identity that society had conditioned you for did not accommodate or invite this kind of creativity. What did you do next?

I continued to read everything I could find that might free me from this depression. Finally, I found Abraham Maslow's book *Toward a Psychology of Being*. He was a prominent research psychologist at the time, and he became the next great meme-maker to change my life. He studied well people rather than sick people. Maslow found that everybody who was successful, creative, joyful, and productive had one thing in common: they were doing chosen work that they found to be both intrinsically self-rewarding and of service to others. He discovered that *self-rewarding action that is simultaneously of service to others* is the key. When you are doing what you love to do and expressing your potential, you experience an inner reward. And by helping others by engaging in this work, you become what he called *self-actualizing*. You are actualizing your own dormant potential by giving it to others who can use it. It is beyond selfishness or selflessness. It is self-fulfillment and indeed self evolution. This was my clue to happiness! Self-rewarding action that you feel is intrinsically valuable to your own growth and also helps others is what makes us happy. I think this idea is a universal truth.

Still, you realized you had not found your vocation yet. You were married, a housewife, a mother of five children—happy with all of that in a way, but underneath it all, you were depressed, you felt some deep call to be something more, do something more. What happened after you read Maslow?

I discovered the next clue: you have to reach out to people who attract you, who inspire you. At that time I'd never met anyone to whom I was attracted in the way I was to Maslow and his work. So, one day I mustered enough courage to call him up. I asked him to lunch, and he actually said yes! So, another principle is: *reach out and be bold*. Don't think it's just going to happen to you by sitting back and waiting.

Further, if you feel depressed, and if you have some sense that there's something in you that hasn't been expressed, then tell yourself: It's a signal that *the universe inside me is pushing me to act towards something more.* Give your frustration a plus sign rather than a negative sign! Rather than wondering, "What's wrong with me?" ask, "What wants to be born in me?" This shifts your focus toward what is emerging that you can now bring forth.

Again, you've got to find at least one other person who attracts you and can recognize you. You have to be seen by somebody as *who you really are.* I was very fortunate that I was actually seen by Abraham Maslow as my own essential self. At that memorable lunch, we had a wonderful conversation, and I told him I was seeking to know what was the meaning of our new power that was good. I said I wanted to make contact with people who could help answer this question. To my surprise, he told me he wanted to give me his list of 300 people to contact who were in his Eupsychian ("good souls") Network. It had taken many years for him to find these people. He said something was needed to bring them together, and this question would help.

It was obvious that Maslow and I had a shared purpose. I still have the note he sent to me after he had a serious heart attack written on a torn piece of green steno paper. It said: "Barbara, never give in. You represent life."

Of course, you have to bear in mind that there was no "human potential movement" in those days! The issue of personal growth was not in the air as it is now. Nevertheless, I wrote a letter to all 300 people on Maslow's list, asking them, "What do you think is the next step forward for the future good? I think it's a birth of a cocreative, evolving humanity." I called this publication *The Center Letter* and offered to print excerpts of their letters of response in the next edition. People sent more names and gave the *Letter* to their friends. The *Letter* traveled all over the world. In that one gesture, with one carefully prepared and well-articulated letter combined with one attracted person, Abraham Maslow, I put myself into a larger community. My new life began.

All these steps were necessary to get my work started. I was a pioneer. At that time, few of us knew about our greater human potential, much less anything about the impending global crises. Now, in 2012, millions of us are engaged in personal growth, spirituality, health and wellness, and so much more. People in general are now far more aware of the threats to life that we now face, and many are active in movements of all kinds to heal the earth, free people from injustice, activate peace, generate new energy sources—in general, evolve consciousness. A vast amount of crucial information necessary for the Planetary Birth is now out there, along with the growing awareness that the crises we are facing are accelerating exponentially. Given our social reality, anyone who would like to be awakened today has a far better time of it than any of us could in the fifties, especially women before the feminist movement came along.

Yes, an easier time indeed. Thank goodness. But I think the formula is the same. I think you just said you took three steps. The first step is finding your vocation, figuring out what was inside you that you have to give. Is that right?

Not exactly. The first step is understanding the feeling of frustration, discontent, that nagging lack of meaning in your life. This feeling of dissonance is what initially awakens us. Again, you can interpret that feeling as a signal, not of depression, but rather that *something more wants to be expressed* through you. Ironically, you discover that the depression is a sign that you are waking up. Not everybody has to go through that, but most people are inclined to change when something is really not working or when they hunger for something more.

Tuning in to Our "Compass of Joy"

And then reaching out for others, identifying what you're attracted to seems an important step. Your connection with Abraham Maslow was a big force for you. You were attracted to the light that he radiated especially because he was studying people who were healthy. He had good news. He was another bearer of good news besides yourself. That's a really important part of the equation. It was a one-in-a-million chance perhaps, but look what happened to you: you got Abraham Maslow to have lunch with you.

Yes, and it doesn't have to be someone like Abraham Maslow. It could be an organization or a person next door who's doing something that interests you. You are looking for people who awaken something that excites and attracts you. It's the relationships you create that are important to this process. You're looking for resonance, affinity, and coherence, like I felt with you, Jan. When you started to talk to me, something woke up in me. I was feeling a frustration because I wasn't sure how to make this story accessible to millions of people. Within ten minutes of you asking me what I wanted to say in the book, there was a download pouring out of me that was very coherent.

The lesson here is that you have to notice what attracts you and pay attention to what is happening. How do you tell? The signal is an inner feedback signal I call "the compass of joy." The compass turns on when you are with a person who attracts you to give your gift in such a way that the other person is able to give more of *their* gift with you. You feel a creative synergy when you join your creativity with that of someone who also wants to create something new. "Synergy" means creating a whole greater than the sum of the parts. It takes time, attention, and nurturing. Almost all creative people join with others to cocreate.

However, when the compass shuts down and you feel stress and discomfort, that's a signal. Stop. Take a breath. Ask, "What is my heart's desire?" Be silent and allow your heart's desire to show up. Sometimes it's just a whisper. You have to ask and cultivate deep listening to become receptive to the responses coming through your heart. And that's why I find it very helpful to write these responses in my personal journal.

My practice for many years has been to sit in silence, to do a meditation, and then to feel the impulse of creativity coming up through my solar plexus and through my heart. It lodges itself in my upper heart where I feel what I call "vocational arousal"—what I am born to do in this world—and perhaps, also receive some hints of how to take a next step in that direction. Seeking inner guidance in these ways is an essential spiritual practice.

In the movie *The Secret,* it's all about what you want to get. My discovery of the secret is that it's more about finding out what you want to *give.* It's discovering what you want to give others and giving it to somebody who needs it. That's where true joy and happiness lie. *That's* the secret.

Entering the "Inner Sanctuary"

And by the same token, giving is receiving. If we frame it in such a way that we are asking ourselves "What do I have to give?"—then we're inviting ourselves to manifest what is being born through us. In order to discover this, you've told us about your practice of journaling while seeking guidance. Do you have a spiritual practice other than journaling?

I didn't have *any* practice for many, many years except writing in my journal. To be more specific, I write out as clearly as I can in my journal exactly what the situation is, such as: *This is happening . . .* or, *I have this question,* or *this problem.* Then I stop thinking and develop a poised mind and remain open to what is emerging. That means *not* going to sleep, and *not* going into profound meditation. It's deep listening. What seems to come through is higher mind, deeper intelligence, wisdom. Then I write without editing myself, without allowing my mental mind to interrupt the process. Often I find that the higher mind is much wiser than my mental mind, or what Ashok Gangadean calls the "ego-mental" self in his essay later in the book.

As my practice developed, I became excited by what this writing was revealing. I remember times when I was inspired to do large-scale things: *Barbara, go out and do this!* or *Go do that!* When I was feeling the oneness, the peace, the wholeness from that higher guidance, I felt wise and assured. But now I also ran into a new challenge: When I went out to do the work, I soon lost connection with my higher guidance. I would feel anxious, compulsive, negative, and overwhelmed with a sense of failing, no matter how hard I worked. Yet I couldn't stop working! I was being more compulsive than creative, and felt no real sense of fulfillment or joy, no matter how apparently successful I was. I realized at those times that I needed to stop and go within.

I eventually decided to get up very early each morning and do a new kind of meditation. I created what I now call an "Inner Sanctuary," a place of deep quiet, protected from my phone, computer, and "to do" list. In that space I did a simple meditation to quiet my mind. I then placed the attention of what I now call my "local egoic self" on the experience of the wise self, the Essential Self, my true nature.

In time, that feeling of love, peace, wisdom, and oneness started to affect my compulsive self. I experienced this higher self as an actual frequency of love coming into my heart. I was opening to love. I eventually discovered that the local self, the egoic self, wanted to be in the presence of my loving essence.

The Inner Sanctuary experience became a safe place for the compulsive self as I continued the meditation practice. I could rest in peace every morning, dwelling with the higher self until I realized that the *higher self is me*. It was clear that this was not some great external being; it's my own essence.

Gradually, I began to feel the bliss of union of my local egoic self with the deeper, spiritual, divine self. I felt the vibration of love filling my heart. The longer I stayed in the sanctuary, the more I felt the union. I soon learned that whatever I put my attention on grows.

I began to integrate the local separated self with my own essence. And now, my practice every day is to go into the silence and get in touch with the feeling of essence, my true nature. Then I bring my egoic self right into that invisible field, where it is naturally infused with the energy and love of the deeper Essential Self. The egoic self, in fact, falls in love with its own essence! Gradually, my egoic self has become infused with the higher self and reflects more of the peace, love, and goodness of its essence. I have become more able to carry out the higher guidance. This is a gradual, lifelong practice of integration.

Is there a component of this work that involves practicing with others?

Yes! The next key step is to find a friend or two and invite them to create what I call a resonant core group or evolutionary circle with you. These days, we are also calling them "Shift Circles." Your circle creates a sacred space as each member enters into the Inner Sanctuary, where each of you can resonate and share with each other—essence to essence.

"Resonance" in this sense means echoing back the Essential Self in one another. This process of two or more joining in resonance serves to deepen each person's

Essential Self. Essence is creative and always present, holding the code of your deeper life purpose and your gift to the larger world. More will be said about resonant circles, also known as "Evolutionary Shift Circles," later in the book.

We're talking about a spiritual practice, a way to truly merge with our higher selves. Would you speak a little more about what occurred for you when you experienced that merging? It's quite a shift for some of us to realize that what we are talking with, when we practice, is our own inner Self.

This is a very important point. I am thinking of a comment from Joseph Chilton Pierce, who said that we have projected our own potentialities on to various gods. It is a profound mystery that Spirit is actually our own essence. This mystery is only realized by a steady, progressive shifting from ego to essence.

In any case, by following this discovery process through daily practice, my deeper life purpose was gradually revealed; it is for me to be a communicator of evolutionary potential. That's a very big project! Actually, it's far more than a project; it's my *vocation of destiny*—the feeling that this is what I am born to do.

So, the question for each of us is, "What is *my* unique way of expressing *my* essence that is both self-rewarding and of service to others?" And, in addition: "How can I *remain* in essence while I am actually making my contribution?"

It sounds like it goes back to Abraham Maslow. The question we need to ask ourselves is, "What is the best way and the most joyful way I can express my essence?" Once we know that, and do that, we are true to ourselves and our soul's mission. Like that quote from the Kabbalah, "We receive the light, then we impart the light. Thus we repair the world."

Yes, exactly. In my practice every morning, I really feel my essence come in. I feel the Impulse of Evolution dwelling in my heart as my own impulse to be more fully who I am. Then I directly ask my Essential Self what it is moving toward that it wants to express through me. What makes this attractive is that it is not my ego trying to get something done; it's my essence giving freely out of its love and creativity.

When you are living your life from this place, people feel love radiating through you. They are attracted to your expression of creativity. It's less about teaching other people and more about the embodiment of essence as it expresses itself through you. When that happens, a sense of fulfillment comes in, a feeling of joy. It's not a sacrifice. You are cocreating in order to become more complete, more whole. I've often thought that since God put joy into the act of *reproducing* the species by creating sexual union, a profound joy can be found in *evolving* the species through a joining of genius.

Using "Vocational Arousal" and "Suprasex" to Cocreate

One of the things that I think makes you such a master teacher is your playful approach to something that is profoundly serious. You have coined a couple of phrases that are recognized by thousands of people around the world. One, which you mentioned already, is "vocational arousal." The other is your notion of "suprasex." I believe these are two essential components of the Planetary Birth, as each of us is born to join with others so we can experience and express higher levels of creativity. Am I understanding it properly?

Yes, you are. As I said, nature invented the joy of sexuality to ensure the procreation of the species. But it now also offers us "suprasexuality" to encourage us to cocreate with others, in order to evolve ourselves and our world. In sexuality we join our genes to have a baby; in suprasexuality, we join our genius to give birth to more of ourselves and our greater work in the world. We are shifting from procreation to cocreation, from self-reproduction to self-evolution.

Evolution's secret is that it won't let out more creativity unless there's some resonance between two or more. Nature's pattern is to create deeper resonance and cooperation to conceive the new. Something new is being conceived by us through the fusion of genius. Nature is attracting us to where we can best cocreate because it always wants to realize more potential. Suprasex is one of her ingenious ways to get us to do more cocreating right now!

Think of the miracle of sperm and egg: there's that one noble little sperm that gets into the egg, and then look what happens! In the same way, when two people join genius, there's a fusion of creativity. A conception occurs through the joining of genius. Of course, you don't just join your genius with *anybody*, any more than you would just have sex with anybody.

So, again, the joining of genius usually comes through vocational arousal. You reach out to find someone who attracts you with whom you feel a potential fusion of genius. When that happens, it's a signal from nature to spend more time together to explore what wants to be created. If you feel that vocational arousal is occurring with someone else, something lights up inside both of you, and you experience a feeling that "this is it." I think it's intriguing, Jan, that the way our conversation is unfolding in telling this story is itself a living example of vocational arousal and cocreativity.

Right. And, as you evolve, synchronicities increase. You were struggling to write about cocreativity and you were working alone—just at the moment I was walking through your door to visit my friend Judy Cauley, who lives and works with you as your colleague and thought partner. After our initial conversation about the book Birth 2012 and Beyond, I got excited to work with you in bringing the book into form. This is also a beautiful example of synchronicity. Once people identify what gift they have for the world and are ready to give it, the world opens up like a portal and draws them into a series of meetings and adventures that take them to a higher level.

It's true, Jan, and another insight here is that synchroncity itself is a sign of a deeper pattern within the universe. The deeper you go in your sensitivity to your own essence, the more synchronicities occur in life.

And here's another important observation about the evolutionary process: We must be sensitive to what is working and what is *not* working. There is always a signal within you to let you know what is not working. You need to pay attention to that signal. It is telling you that something *else* wants to work. In situations like that, stay open to the synchronicities that occur without any plan or apparent cause. It might be a surprise phone call from someone you have been thinking of, or a creative inspiration that "pops up" in a conversation with an unlikely ally. Synchronicities may reveal a new connection, a new insight, or an important signal about how to express your creativity in a new way to engage an impasse.

Chapter 3

The New Myth
and the New Memes

Barbara, what were some of your other early influ-
ences that led you to your discovery of the Planetary
Birth process?

My conception of the Planetary Birth was first awakened
in me when I read Teilhard de Chardin's great work *The*
Phenomenon of Man. In this and his other books, he
asserts that the process of creation is sacred, and he brilliantly theorizes that evolution has a direction toward an
ultimate goal, which he called the "Omega Point."

According to Teilhard's "Law of Complexity/Con-
sciousness," as a living system evolves and becomes
more complex, it jumps in consciousness and freedom, as
demonstrated by the fact that cells evolved to eventually
become animals and animals then gave rise to humans.
He also saw that as the world developed a complex biosphere able to support human evolution, it then evolved
a noosphere, or mind-sphere—the "thinking layer" of
Earth. As humans organized themselves into ever more

complex networks of thoughtful and loving relationships, the noosphere would grow proportionally.

Teilhard foresaw that at some point, that thinking layer
—the higher level of consciousness and communications
around the Earth—would get its "collective eyes." This
would occur when humankind as a whole connected, as he
said, heart with heart, and center with center. He called this
great awakening of love the "Christification of the Earth."

Teilhard de Chardin also taught that one day we will
awaken as a whole planet and know ourselves as one
planetary body. That's the basis of my Planetary Birth
vision that came later.

*It sounds like Teilhard de Chardin's work had a large
personal impact on you.*

I fell in love with Teilhard. He awoke my evolutionary
soul. Reading Teilhard gave me a sense of purpose way
beyond my personal life. It inspired in me an awareness
of the direction of life itself toward higher consciousness, more harmonious order, and greater freedom. His
perspective went far beyond what the current culture was
saying in those days. For example, the existentialists, like
Sartre and Camus, claimed there was no intrinsic purpose
in life, except what you projected on to it. The materialistic
scientists believed that the universe itself was an accident
that would eventually wind down to an inevitable heat
death. The post-modernists taught that there is no story or
governing myth, and argued that everything is relative and
nothing is more true than anything else. By contrast, what
I heard from Teilhard is that the universe has direction,
meaning, and purpose! Through his vision, I could see that
I am in the universe, and the universe is in me.

I was profoundly excited to participate in this evolutionary potentiality, and I soon realized that that's where
I want my creativity to be focused! Suddenly, my identity
took a quantum leap from being a depressed housewife

to becoming the universe in person! My heart's desire to express more, know more, participate more was not "neurotic" as I was labeled in the 1950s. It was *evolutionary*. With that awareness, I experienced my own "conception" as a universal human. Teilhard's larger vision awakened my own greater creativity.

How does Teilhard speak to you today, given the very different conditions we now face on planet Earth?

My reading of Teilhard's work was a primary factor leading to my vocational arousal in the fifties and early sixties. Teilhard was never published by the Catholic Church in his lifetime. Yet the amazing thing is that his understanding of love connecting us heart to heart and center to center through the noosphere is actually happening now. This was his prophecy for us: "Someday after mastering winds, waves, tides and gravity, we shall harness the energies of **love**, and then, for the second time in the history of the world, humans will discover **fire**." This is now occurring! A variety of measures have confirmed that empathy is increasing and spirituality is deepening. Millions are awakening to our crises. In his important book *Blessed Unrest,* Paul Hawken wonders, "How is it the largest movement in the world came into being and no one saw it coming?"

We also see Teilhard's vision of the noosphere unfolding through the vehicles of electronic connectivity, the Internet, and social media. Over four billion cell phones are in use worldwide as of this writing! We now know that people connecting via Facebook and cell phones can mobilize masses to overthrow dictators. They can *become* the news themselves as in the Occupy movement and other social movements seeking to create more participatory democracy and economic justice. The noosphere is connecting us from within, while electronic communications are linking us from without. The "innernet" and the Internet are converging!

My sense is that everybody's life purpose is enormously enhanced when they feel they can contribute to a greater, transcendent whole—if they can awaken beyond themselves to the vision of a major planetary shift.

The power that we've gained through understanding nature is the power to destroy or evolve the world. Yet the question remains, how are we going to evolve the world? I think we are going to do it by connecting with the intelligence of our collective "global brain." The synergy of love and knowledge gives us the wisdom needed to solve almost any problem. We may be on the threshold of a nonlinear, exponential interaction of novel elements in society. Just as problems are growing exponentially, so is the connectivity of innovation and creativity.

Is this what gives you the hope that, in time, we can experience the planetary awakening?

Yes. The possibility of an actual planetary awakening or Birth experience is not a mythical fantasy. It is a natural phase-change that is already happening. The evolutionary patterns that are leading us to the Birth are apparent in our 13.7-billion-year evolutionary history.

Let's put it this way: Any planet that has developed a biosphere and a noosphere will be able to either destroy itself through misuse of its new power, especially technological, or evolve itself by the loving use of the very same powers. We are the first humans on planet Earth to have that choice. If we continue to overgrow in the womb of Earth, we can render ourselves and much of Earth life extinct. The important concept of conscious evolution is the awareness that—in the face of this threat—we must evolve by choice, not chance. To "be causal," as I like to put it, is a powerful meme for all time!

As I earlier noted, we know that if the birth of a baby doesn't happen in time, it will die and even cause the death of its mother. Our planetary crisis of Birth will not have a positive ending without enough of us activating our creativity, hope, and connectivity. The fate of Earth is in our hands. It's up to *us* to nurture this Birth.

A New Myth for Our Times

Some suggest that when people stop believing in the prevailing myths of the time, the culture begins to disintegrate. There are so many signs of disintegration in our culture, so many of our myths are failing us now. They are not big enough to hold up to our increasing levels of intelligence and our increasing demands for integrity. The old beliefs are simply too small for these times. I feel like you're presenting a new myth to the culture that we can believe in. Do you have that sense?

Indeed! The last great myth took root during the Renaissance—the myth of progress through knowledge, science, democracy, and technology. We believed it. And there was good reason to believe it. In many ways life did get better for millions of people. But the modern world, or at least the Western world, has lost its "meta-narrative." Its "big story," this myth of progress, began to collapse after the two world wars in which tens of millions of people were killed by the most sophisticated nations and technologies. This culminated with America dropping the atomic bombs on Japan showing that we could actually destroy the world. In recent decades, it was followed by a set of mounting global crises we are now facing everyday.

The myth of progress had almost disappeared completely in academia while I was going to college in 1947–1951. And, other than the fundamentalist embrace of the literal interpretation of Biblical scripture, no new myths have arisen in modern times that give us a sense of meaning, direction, and hope. Since then, we have been living without a myth or a large enough vision and context to give us a shared sense of oneness, purpose, and direction.

But here is the good news: There *is* a new meta-narrative. An all-inclusive new Universe Story is emerging under the surface of the old news of crises. It is the *evolutionary worldview*. This new meta-narrative is not yet anchored in our existing religions, universities, or political and corporate power structures, although it is bubbling up in individuals, small groups, books, teachings, projects, and thousands of organizations everywhere.

Cosmosgenesis and the "Three Cs"

The new myth I'm presenting began with the convergence of three elements: cosmosgenesis, new crises, and new capacities—what I like to call the "Three Cs."

The first "C" is *cosmogenesis*, which refers to the discovery of the way the universe has been evolving for billions of years. It was only in the mid-sixties that two scientists, Arno Penzius and Robert Wilson, identified background radiation from the original moment of creation—the Big Bang—and were able to extrapolate backward in time to those first instants of creation. Only since then do we understand that the universe is not static or eternal. With the story of the Big Bang, the great flaring forth, and the evolution of the universe, we now understand that "From No Thing at All" has come "Everything That Was, Is Now, and Will Be."

Our discovery of cosmosgenesis now allows us to place ourselves *in* the story, *as* the story evolving through us. The first "C," cosmogenesis, is the basis of the new worldview, the context and the framework for all Earth life. As we discussed before, this is subjectively experienced as the inner impulse in each of us, motivating us to be more, to do more, to love more, to know more, and to participate more in serving others and society. The Impulse of Evolution, the motivating force behind billions years of evolution, is active in each of us now. *We are the universe in person!* You and I are how cosmogenesis shows up as a person. The evolutionary process that impels the rise of complexity and ever more intelligent life forms—from atoms to molecules, cells, animals, humans, great avatars, and geniuses—is in us and motivating us right now.

The second "C" is new crises brought on by our over-populating, our polluting, our war-making with weapons of mass destruction, and the gap between the haves and have-nots, all of which could lead to a global catastrophe. The crises of our time are evolutionary drivers that spur us to evolve beyond where we are today—or die!

Right now our whole social system is withering, leadership is faltering and failing, and problems are escalating exponentially, giving us very little time to change. At the very same moment, millions of pioneering souls are seeking a higher order of life, that is, new structures and not just new projects. They are searching out or they are creating new systems and innovations in health, education, environment, energy, business. In the great 13.7-billion-year tradition of nature itself, these innovations are creating the conditions for an evolutionary leap.

They are creating what the complexity theorists call a "strange attractor" toward a higher order culture. This attractor—which offers greater consciousness, freedom, and compassion—is emerging subtly everywhere, but is not yet coordinated, connected, or visible. We have not yet "connected the dots."

But remember, as John Stewart writes in The Evolutionary Manifesto, nature selects for what cooperates best. This is a multi-billion year trend! As Laszlo tells us, "Small fluctuations in a sea of social chaos can jump the whole system to a higher order." We can be part of that small fluctuation. The morphogenetic field of consciousness, creativity, and compassion that we are building will enable us to make the quantum leap in time.

Coming to Terms with Our New Capacities

The third "C" is *capacities*. Our new technical capacities, such as biotechnology, nuclear power, nanotechnology, quantum computing, robotics, and space travel, are radical evolutionary powers that are dangerous in our current state of self-centered, separation consciousness. Yet, at the same time, we are achieving new levels of collective heart-intelligence and global coherence at the noospheric stage of evolution. Our new capacities are the growing powers of a young, universal species. If we consider that we are continuing to evolve and indeed may be entering the next stage of evolution itself, these new powers might be what we actually need to become a universal species.

We have been brought to this new threshold and worldview of conscious evolution through the convergence of cosmogenesis, new crises, and new capacities. We now have our new myth, our new story—the story of the universe. This is a tremendous shift in our worldview from believing that we lived within a static universe, to seeing ourselves in an evolving and expanding universe in which we have an intrinsic part to play.

In this video, entitled "What Is Conscious Evolution?" Barbara fully explains the concept of conscious evolution.

This new story also reveals to us that Earth is a living organism. With evolutionary eyes we can see that we are being animated and coordinated by the very same process that brought atom to atom, cell to cell, and led to the appearance of an endless array of forms of life over billions of years. This process is now connecting us on a planetary scale. The noosphere is knitting together our global brain/mind/heart minute-by-minute. We realize that our creativity and our commitment to love is the real power that can bring us to a new future, a new world, a new hope, a new humanity. This is the *real* news and the new myth for our time.

The Emergence of Homo universalis

You have also stated that, as the new story arises, so does a new type of person. Teilhard talked about Homo progressivus. *You speak and write about* Homo universalis. *I think that you are both trying to share an image of a new and higher being and my guess is that these are two names for the same new species. Can you talk more about your idea of the Universal Human?*

Surely, but let me first backtrack again and talk about what initially inspired this image as well as my belief in the possibility of us becoming a universal species. This quest started in 1948 during my junior year of college in Paris when I met Earl Hubbard, an artist and the man I married.

I first met him while having lunch alone one day in a little café on the Left Bank called Chez Rosalie. It was a cold November day. I walked into the café, drawn by the warmth of the fire and the aroma of chestnuts roasting. I sat down at one of the little wooden tables. I was in my beret, smoking a Gaulois cigarette, and ordered a half bottle of red wine (trying to be an "existentialist"). The door opened and in walked a handsome American.

He had to sit opposite me at the only empty place at the table. His name was Earl Hubbard.

After a while, I offered him a bit of my red wine, raised up my courage, and asked my question: "What do you think is the meaning of our new powers that is good?"

He amazed me by saying, "I am an artist, and I am seeking a new image of man commensurate with our powers to shape the future." He went on to tell me that when a culture loses its story, it loses its greatness. He gave a wonderful portrayal of Michelangelo's sculpture *David*, describing its image of a beautiful, integrated, almost divine-looking human hero, and said this sculpture offered the last great example of a dignified human self-image. He then pointed out how modern art demonstrates the disintegration of that image over time, as could be seen in the works of Manet, Monet, Pissarro, Picasso, Jackson Pollock, and others. Earl concluded: "We've lost our story, we've lost our self-image, and recovering it is the work of the artist." I knew then and there I would marry him!

Earl and I had five children while he worked as an artist, seeking this new expression. Finally, at a certain point, we began our journey of cocreation. Every morning after I drove the children to school, I returned home and got out my tape recorder for our "breakfast dialogues."

Out of these deep and inspiring conversations, we pieced together the new story of our Birth.

It was the time of the Apollo program. We envisioned ourselves becoming physically universal. We projected ourselves forward, becoming part of what Earl called the new "cultural body of humankind." As he wrote in his (now out of print) book, *The Search Is On*:

> From the deep dark womb of evolution
> Humanity has been born.
> Our eyes and ears are opening,
> We listen and understand.

As one body we study the new description
Of the forces of Creation
Gleaned for us by science.
In the light of our dawning awareness, we seek
Deeper contact with the Creative Intention
And the role we can play in universal affairs.

Earl and I began to realize that humankind was literally being born as a universal species, spiritually, socially, as well as technologically. We started our dialogues by asking, "What happens to us humans, born into a rapidly maturing noosphere in a universe that is designed to foster ever more intelligent life? What is the next step after *Homo habilis, Homo erectus, Homo neanderthal,* and *Homo sapiens*?" "*Homo universalis*" is the name we gave to what we could see ourselves becoming. These discussions were the foundation of my evolutionary journey.

All these years later, in 2012, we, as a species, are finally entering the age of conscious evolution and the mass appearance of this new type of human. As universal humans, we are consciously integrating our social, spiritual, technological, and scientific capacities with our highest aspirations to create a world that works for everyone. We can now imagine living in a more synergistic, cocreative society with extended intelligence, extended life span, extended creativity, the development of space, tapping into new clean energies, and much more. It was Albert Einstein who told us, "Imagination is everything. It is the preview of life's coming attractions."

Since we are just now entering this new era, and have never been here before, what lessons do we have to guide us into the unknown?

To discover some lessons we first have to *gain evolutionary eyes.* The historical time frame of the last few generations is too short to provide us with these lessons.

With evolutionary eyes, we gain the perspective of deep time past. We can look back at the whole story of evolution as our story. This perspective reveals core, evolutionary lessons to guide us in crossing the gap from breakdown to breakthrough: As stated earlier, *crises precede transformation.* Before every quantum change in our evolutionary history problems occurred—limits to growth, stagnation, unmanageable complexities, impending catastrophes. From the perspective of the present, crises look like mistakes, deadly errors in the system. But, with evolutionary eyes, *problems are considered evolutionary drivers*—vital stimulants that trigger astounding innovations, which in turn bring out new potentials and capture them in stable form, producing absolute newness. Whatever emerges will be a new life form. We are the first humans to be given this opportunity to participate in the conscious evolution of humanity and Earth. Each of us is needed as an agent of conscious evolution. Each of us is needed to contribute our part to cocreating a new world and a new humanity.

Yet another great lesson is that *nature takes jumps through greater synergy,* which I define as the coming together of separate parts to make new whole systems greater than and unpredictable from the sum of its parts. In fact, nature is a hierarchy of synergies. As I stated earlier, nature selects for what cooperates best to evolve life. We learn from biologist Elisabet Sahtouris that when a species is young, it tends to overpopulate, pollute, compete with, and eventually destroy its environment. It either learns to cooperate with itself, its environment, and other species, or it goes extinct. We certainly can see the meaning of these lessons for us!

We also learn how nature has evolved up the chain of complexity into multiple life forms. Nature has demonstrated that it seeks out novel connections during times of crises. As I said, at some point a nonlinear, exponential interaction of new elements occurs and systems jump to a higher order, to a more complex and creative form of life.

Discovering That We Are the News

Do you see these kinds of connections and interactions occurring at this time in our evolutionary story?

We are right at that point now. There are innovations and breakthroughs in every field that are not yet fully connected, yet our noosphere is actually connecting us through its very rapid interaction. We can anticipate moving toward our convergence and coherence as a whole planetary system. It is the universal tendency within us pressing us forward. With an evolutionary perspective we can see that we are moving toward a new future, an unknown future that we are just now imagining.

You often use the phrase "gentling the birth," and I'm wondering what that has to do with what we're talking about here?

Well, it could be a violent birth. It is impossible to continue overgrowing in the womb of Earth. We are destroying life itself; we are destroying untold numbers of species, all of which leads to catastrophe. We could go through the coming transition with hundreds of millions dying, with enormous forces unleashed against each other as we fight for food and water, and, in the process, damage the intellectual and spiritual heritage of humanity. Birth is always beautiful, mysterious, and dangerous.

To gentle the Planetary Birth, we can learn from the experience of natural childbirth. During childbirth a mother gets to a point where she says, "I can't do this, it's too much." Then a good doula or midwife says, "But you're already doing it!" This encourages the mother to relax into the birthing process. The doula helps her to realize that within her is an "inner mother," a universal mother, that knows just what to do, even though the mother suffering in labor doesn't know she knows. She must trust the mystery at work within the birthing process.

So, it's important to realize that during the suffering of these planetary birth crises, there is an Impulse of Evolution within us that *does* know what to do. It has been evolving life for billions of years! We *do* have the resources, the technology, the global noosphere, and the lessons of evolution to help us cocreate a world that does work for everyone and all Earth life. The question to ask is, "Do we have the will and courage to evolve by choice, not chance?"

Clearly this choice involves both head and heart. What is needed to open our hearts so that we will choose conscious evolution?

These days, when there are crises in the world, we watch them live in the mass media. This activates our heart connection. We see people suffering, dying, killing each other, homes blown away. We feel the pain of others as our own. Our hearts open, and we send help. We care for each other. This level of heart connection across the world is radically new. It is also what Teilhard de Chardin predicted would happen when the noosphere got its "collective eyes," and we connect heart with heart and center with center. Our worldview has changed forever.

When we see a great crisis hit, and when we see people being heroic in the face of it, these images embolden us. When you see somebody being courageous, it's much more likely that you'll be courageous. Our pioneering ancestors crossed oceans in desperate conditions toward an unknown future that held the promise of more freedom, more possibilities, and a new beginning. This is an enduring image. We are now the new pioneers, and people are drawn to give our gifts, to be creative, to move toward our unknown future. What gives us hope is our trust in the Impulse of Evolution continuing on its path toward higher consciousness and greater freedom. Even now, our suffering and pain are activating the empathy, the creativity, and courage needed for us to mature as a species. This is the *new* news! This is the great work of our time.

Yes, and that's probably what you mean by "we become the news." We gather evidence of our successes in the world and no longer leave it up to the old media that still seems to be operating on the principle "if it bleeds, it leads." That's so old. It should be, "If it feeds, it leads." If it feeds the soul, feeds our collective eyes, feeds our imagination—then it should lead.

The mainstream media is like an infant's nervous system. It communicates pain and hunger, and then puts us to sleep. In contrast, our new media via the Internet is connecting us through personal relationships, friendships, and collaborative projects emerging everywhere.

There is a new image emerging for us now. The early images from the space program of astronauts looking at Earth from space transformed our worldview forever. However, those pictures did not show the people of Earth, our culture, our arts, our systems, and the growing noosphere. It's one thing to see the planet as a geographic entity, but it's another to ask—what does our "thought field" look like? What does the field of Spirit on the planet look like? How does the noosphere look and feel?

We need a new art form that evokes our passion about becoming a new humanity that opens our collective eyes to see the invisible becoming visible. The image of a Planetary Birth experience offers us a shared vision of who we are becoming as a very young universal humanity. Birth 2012 could be our epiphany—our great transformational experience.

Embracing the "Great Birthing Process"
of Our Time

I just had an experience while you were talking of imagining the Planetary Birth Day, and I became teary all of a sudden. I'm overwhelmed with joy already, just imagining what we will see on our computers and TVs: people from Siberia to South America, the First Nations, Polynesians from the Pacific Islands, and children from Harlem to Hungary beaming and singing "Happy Birthday" to the new Earth.

Yes, and as we discussed earlier, we've already had a couple of similar occasions. We've had the lunar landing in 1969. We had a foretaste of this joy during the new millennium celebrations. Do you remember how they started at one part of Earth and you could see the celebrations all around the world? What were they celebrating? Did they even know?

My sense of it was we were welcoming the great unknown, the blank slate of a new millennium, a new chance to get it right this time.

We may get it right, but we also know that there are no experts to tell us how to make it through to the next stage of evolution, beyond 2012. There are no elders to show us the way. It is becoming clear to more and more of us that we can come through the global crises only if we have a new consciousness and a commitment to love. The global crises are awakening love, empathy, and compassion on a global scale. This is the new news, the new story of our emergence as a cocreative humanity that must be told in a compelling and coherent way everywhere: The good news is—*we are consciously creating a new future!*

I think what you're saying is that it's already happening. And a small percentage of us know it so powerfully while many are sleeping right through it. How can it happen for more of us?

The reason for Birth 2012 is to awaken enough people to this amazing good news and evoke the exact spirit that brought tears to your eyes, Jan. It's what Teilhard de Chardin called the "flame of expectation"; it might lie dormant in us now, but it never goes out. We don't see what we are becoming. We don't see what is already happening. We don't see the natural direction of evolution toward higher consciousness and greater freedom. We don't understand that problems are evolutionary drivers. We don't see that our crisis is a birth! And, we're not just going to get it by dying and being reborn, or in life after death, or through a near death experience. In the words of Teilhard, "We must discover fire for the second time!"

To fully awaken, we need a shared peak experience or a mass spiritual experience of expanded reality. Mystics and visionaries have had such experience all through human history, but it has never been a communal experience. Widespread spiritual experiences of our wholeness, oneness, and goodness could become a collective awakening during our Planetary Birth process and celebration.

I am interested in knowing how you understand the birthing process of a new Earth and a universal humanity. What does that look like for you?

I see the birthing process as the unfolding story of creation. Our conception originated in the Void, the Field of All Possibilities—the mind of the cosmos—God—and has been manifesting through billions of years of cosmic evolution. This Great Birthing Process is now emerging among us as the gestation phase of evolution barely perceptible at the horizon of our current awareness, too original to be fully experienced except by those with eyes to see and ears to hear the faint signals of the evolving humanity. These signals are as difficult to recognize as the first cells in the seas of Earth as they emerged out of the prebiotic world, or the early humans who first appeared out of the animal world. Now, we seek to understand what is being born out of the world of current *Homo sapiens sapiens*: a universal, empathetic, and spiritually motivated humanity becoming conscious of the evolutionary processes that are creating us, and ever more capable of cocreating with them. Conscious evolution explores the great mystery story of creation which is already unfolding within and beyond us as the birth of the next phase of evolution. Our ultimate purpose is the evolution of our species to full humanhood, co-evolving with nature and cocreating with Spirit. This is my understanding of the birthing process of a universal humanity.

Thank you, Jan, for engaging me in this deep conversation about *my* personal journey in conscious evolution. It was the perfect context for what is emerging. I am thrilled to be inviting you and millions of others to join me now in participating in Birth 2012—*our* shared journey into the age of conscious evolution.

The Flame of Expectation

What is this flame of expectation, this growth impulse,
this frustration that urges us to break through
the given pattern of our lives?

What pulls us as though by an irresistible magnet toward each
other, and toward a desirable yet undefined state of being?

Over 13.7 billion years it has continued to draw
atoms to atoms, molecules to molecules, cells to cells—
and now people to people in ever more complex systems.
For this flame is the radiant energy of love!

It is more than our personal love for each other, one by one;
and it is even greater than altruistic love for others.
It is also, and more so, a transpersonal love,
one that senses the fulfillment of one's self
through deep involvement in the evolution of the world
in connection with a Universal Force.

The flame is the attractive and attracted energy
that moves the process—the intention of Creation.

It was ignited at the beginning of Creation,
and it became self-conscious at the dawn of Humanity.

It is now rising higher, kindled by the maturation of science
as it probes the mysteries of the Universe from without.
And, it is kindled by the deepening intuition
of millions attuning to reality from within,
kindled by the dangers pressing upon our species as a whole.

The flame of expectation is igniting us,
animating and attracting us to move beyond
our existing life patterns.

It leads us to do more, to be more, to know more,
and above all to connect more with each other,
to discover what we can do together
that none of us can do isolated and alone.

Do these words resonate as true to you?
Have you experienced yourself as a living part of Creation,
at one with all of nature?
Do you feel drawn to give your gift to the Planetary Shift?

Part 2

PARTICIPATING IN THE BIRTH

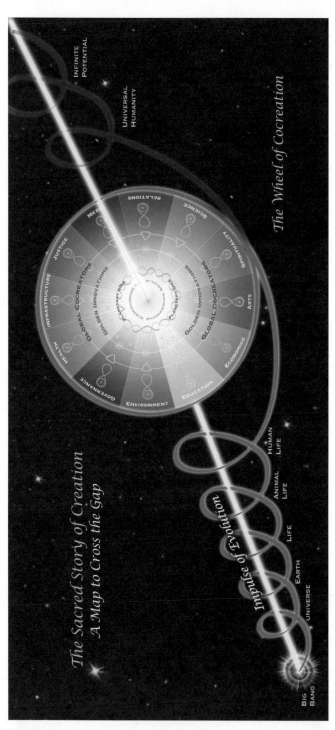

Figure 1: The Sacred Story of Creation. A high-resolution version of this image can be found at Birth2012.com.

Chapter 4

The Map to Cross the Gap

Dear pioneering souls! We are on an unprecedented journey into the planetary birthing process—all of us, of every age, color, background, and faith. In this time of challenge, we are each called upon to contribute our gift to the Great Shift.

And so, the real questions for us become: How do we give our gifts to the Shift at this precise moment in evolutionary time? What can we offer to the uncharted new civilization that is now emerging? How do we activate our own greater potential while also serving the restoration of our world?

These questions lead to other questions: To make it possible to give our gift, how do we make the *inner* shift necessary to end our illusion of separation from each other, from nature, and from Spirit? How do we find our "vocations of destiny"—that is, what we are born to *do* for the Shift? And once we have changed internally and discovered our proper role, how can we contribute to more sustainable and synergistic forms of organization, to more enlightened self-governance at all levels?

To help people answer such questions, I long ago created what I call the "Map to Cross the Gap"—a comprehensive picture of the developmental path that leads us across the chasm between our current breakdowns and our potential for breakthrough. You can see the Map in the color insert under its formal name, the Sacred Story of Creation. (Please see Figure 1 at the beginning of this chapter.) I believe it offers us a big-picture overview of the universal process of creation that we are all part of, enabling us to place our own contributions within a comprehensive evolutionary context.

Taking the Overview Perspective

So, to approach the Map, we begin by gaining *evolutionary eyes*. We adopt an overview perspective that reveals deep-time past and deep-time future, allowing us to see what is happening on the largest scale. We assume a stance that could be called "ec-static"—that is, the act of rising above or outside of things to see the "metapattern" of the whole.

Such a cosmic perspective gives us a new sense of oneness and belonging, and an experience of wonder at the vastness of the developmental path we are on. Simply by seeing Earth from space, some astronauts have had life-changing shifts of consciousness. For astronaut Edgar Mitchell, this shift made him aware that the whole universe is alive, intelligent, and evolving. In the same sense, the overview perspective provided by the Map gives us a *universal* perspective. And by experiencing it, we move toward becoming Universal Humans ourselves. For, as we see reality, so will we act and so will we become. This cosmic perspective provides context for our lives and meaning to our new powers. It changes everything!

Understanding the Map to Cross the Gap

I also call this Map at Figure 1 the Sacred Story of Creation because it represents the cosmic story of universal evolution, while also depicting our current position within it. As you look at the Map with evolutionary eyes, the first thing you notice is that a great Spiral runs through it from one end to the other. The enlarged turn on the Spiral (featuring a multi-colored wheel) is called the Wheel of Cocreation. It symbolizes our moment in the Sacred Story of Creation—our turn on the Spiral—and stands for that point in evolution when humans embrace conscious evolution.

Second, notice that the Map graphically represents how the Spiral originated from the Void, the Mind of God—the Field of infinite possibilities—and then progressed over 13.7 billion years of successful evolution. Evidently, at the moment of the Big Bang, cosmic evolution flared forth from the Origin of Creation, powered by a mysterious process—an Impulse of Evolution that has many names. (I have depicted the Impulse as a white arrow moving upward toward infinite potential, and also passing through the center or "Hub" of the Wheel. It is sometimes referred to as the Core of the Spiral.) From the birth of the universe in the Big Bang, the process of creation emerged as the mystery of evolution spiraling through the formation of the physical universe—energy, matter, galaxies, solar systems, and then localizing as the earth itself, more than four billion years ago.

Earth's newly formed geosphere then provided the basis for the Origin of Life, the next turn on the Spiral, and from here a long procession of evolutionary innovations of great significance emerged. For example, the process of sexual reproduction suddenly appeared, allowing multicellular organisms for the first time to join their genes to create new life. Another critical design innovation was the advent of photosynthesis, which transformed our barren planet into a living biosphere. From these and many other biological leaps came animal life, then human life, and now us—the first generation that is awakening to this whole process of creation.

*In this video, Barbara explains
how to navigate the Map.*

Humanity Enters the Wheel of Cocreation

Humanity has actually been preparing to take its turn on the Spiral for several thousand years through the practices and disciplines of the world's great wisdom traditions, and more recently by virtue of the advent of science and democracy. But only in our generation have we gained the actual powers of cocreation—the ability to become an integral part of the creative process of evolution.

The most fundamental discipline on this path is the practice of a new evolutionary spirituality in which *we shift our relationship with the creative process from creature to cocreator*—that is, from unconscious to conscious evolution. In other words, whereas according to Western tradition we were once seen as "God's creatures," now we have matured sufficiently to become *cocreators* working with and expressing the Impulse of Evolution. To fulfill this entirely new responsibility, we must gain an ever-greater resonance with the metapattern—the Sacred Story of Creation—or, in traditional terms, with the "will of God."

Later in this chapter we will explore how to become more coherent with this metapattern of creation through entering the symbolic Hub of the Wheel of Cocreation. Then, in Chapter 5, we will do so by engaging with the twelve sectors of the Wheel.

Again, bear in mind that the vast potential of our creative genius only became evident in the latter half of the twentieth century, when it become clear that our new scientific, social, and technological abilities had conferred upon us unprecedented powers to affect the evolution of life on Earth. This new reality provided a major impetus for the rise of the worldview of conscious evolution. Our ultimate purpose at this phase of evolution, then, is to learn how to responsibly and ethically manage our new powers as we guide humanity through Birth 2012 and beyond. As I have long pointed out, our deepest heart's desire is to "gentle" our way through this transition.[1]

Embracing Our Developmental Path

Again, the Map is a symbol of the awesome Universe Story becoming conscious within each of us, and *as* each of us, as we enter our turn on the Spiral. When we embrace conscious evolution, this Big Story becomes *our* story, the narrative of our developmental path of cocreation. It provides perspective on the next step of that path: the challenge of the Great Shift.

Each numbered item below illuminates aspects of the Map for you to use as you give your gifts to the Shift in this critical moment. My in-depth teaching about the entire developmental path presented in the Map can be found in the online course entitled Agents of Conscious Evolution, produced by The Shift Network.[2]

1. Remembering Our Story

The first and most important activity linked to the Map is that of simply *remembering* the Sacred Story of Creation. When we remember and then share the new story, we become inspiring guides to others who may be depressed and lost in the myriad of urgent problems that we face every day. In telling this story we become evolutionary agents in the process itself. Remembering the Universe Story immediately gives us a sense of meaning, direction, and purpose, and a more comprehensive vision of our future. Viewing *Our Story*, the first movie in my Humanity Ascending documentary series, will especially assist you in remembering and sharing our new story.[3]

2. Feeling the Core of the Spiral

Next, as we contemplate our story, let us go deeper and *feel* the Core of the Spiral—that is, the Impulse of Evolution or what others call "spirit-in-action." As we discussed earlier, this Impulse is not only animating cosmic evolution, but it is actually running through our hearts, motivating us to be more, do more, love more, and give more. It is the very soul of evolution. It is the consciousness-force that animates matter, life, animal life, and human life that is now becoming conscious of itself *as* us.

The Core of the Spiral with all its powers is now moving through us just as it moved through enlightened and prophetic persons of the past. It is awakening in millions of us, animating us so we can respond creatively to the planetary crisis. It is like bringing God home within ourselves, birthing God in our soul in a way that brings love and creativity into the world. When we feel the Core, we are incarnating what I call the "three Es" of the evolutionary journey:

> *Eternal* Each of us is one with the eternal Source of Life, originating in each moment of creation.
>
> *Embody* We each embody unique expressions of the Impulse of Evolution.
>
> *Emerge* Each of us is the growing edge of evolution becoming ever new.

One way to nurture your awareness of the Core of the Spiral is by using the Evolutionary Chakra Meditation that can be found in my *Evolutionary Communion* guidebook. [4]

3. Resonating in the Hub of the Wheel

When we remember the story and become aware of the Impulse of Evolution coming through our hearts, we symbolically enter the Hub of the Wheel of Cocreation.

While in the Hub, we realize that our moment on the Spiral is not only a time of terrible crises and failure but also the opening of a new phase of human consciousness. We experience hope and a sense of tremendous potentiality. We become aware that our crises are evolutionary drivers that activate new capacities—and that the purpose of these new powers is a more creative and loving life.

The Hub itself is a sacred space; it symbolizes a sanctified place in consciousness for shared revelation of the metapatterns of creation. Here we also cultivate "global heart coherence," a practice that helps us realize that collectively we are the heart and mind of the universe in the unfolding process of creation.

In the Hub, we resonate by resounding back to each other the impulse we each feel within. As we meet in groups, virtually or physically, we tune into the deeper pattern not only within us but within the emerging process of the whole. The Hub can be cultivated to become a field of collective consciousness generated by those resonating within it.

The Hub is also a place where our "inner synergy" or coherence of oneness with the Source joins with the "outer synergy" of our work in the world. The inner shift and the outer shift become one in the Hub of the Wheel. The Hub is both a space in consciousness and a gathering place of pioneering souls engaging in Hub practices, which we explore below.

Evolutionary Hub Practices

In the Hub, we realize we are not alone. We are at home. We are at one with all others who feel in their own hearts this rising tide of love and creativity. In this sacred space, what Teilhard de Chardin called the "flame of expectation" is alive in and animating each of us.

Below are practices we can engage in while "occupying" the space of the Hub. The listing of these techniques begins with my story of how I discovered the essential practice for conscious evolution, what I call the Emergence Process.

1. The Emergence Process:
The Shift from Ego to Essence

On my sixty-ninth birthday, I made a choice that started me on a practice that continues to transform my life. This was when I first began a formal process that I now call "the shift from ego to essence."

The scene was Marin County, California, 1999; it was a cold, rainy January and February. I stayed warm next to my fireplace while a steady rain came down, giving me a feeling of inwardness and protection. I had tasked myself with a huge project: writing a conscious-evolution curriculum for Universal Humans, an educational framework that begins with the Void and covers the origin of the universe and its evolution up to the present and beyond.

My dining room table had been taken over by tidy stacks of books on every phase change in the story of evolution, written by authors whose work had inspired me for many years. The room itself was filled with the presence of the noosphere, the thinking layer of Earth.

In spite of this rich and supportive environment, I found myself compulsive about my work, trapped in an exhausting struggle to get the job done. Although I was urging and encouraging others toward experiencing a positive future for their lives, I couldn't find a place of rest within myself. I knew I had to stop the current momentum of my life in order to make way for something new.

I began each morning before dawn, devoting three hours to silence and solitude. This was long enough to create space for something new to happen. I let there be soft music, candlelight, flowers, and above all, peace and quiet. In that safe inner space, I felt protected, secure, empty, and uninterrupted by my own demands or anyone else's. This "time outside of time" was a place as profound as the quietest monastery or cave, a place I created within and around myself. I now call this place Inner Sanctuary (introduced earlier in the book in my dialogue with Jan Phillips). But even at the thought of doing this, my compulsive, egoic "local self" was prickling. I was bombarded by its loud complaint: "We don't have time; we'll never get the curriculum done." My driven local self always felt behind, no matter what time I woke up and began my work.

But I persisted. Every morning, I simply sat in silence, open and empty, listening to the crackling fire and the rain drumming softly on my roof. I offered my burdens and responsibilities as sacrifices at the threshold of the Inner Sanctuary, literally laying them at the entrance before I entered into my meditation. I imagined myself as a pilgrim in front of a temple, purifying myself before entering. When the compulsive local self prodded me with "You forgot to call so-and-so!" or "What are you going to have for lunch?" I resisted, no matter how magnetic the pull. I felt like the mythological Odysseus, strapped to the mast of his ship to prevent himself from succumbing to the temptation of the Sirens. My egoic, obsessive need to be working was my temptation. I let it go by.

Within the Inner Sanctuary, I created a special place for my journal writing and a quiet time following my meditation to gain more intimate access to the wise and beloved inner voice, the Essential Self, that has guided me all my life. This was a voice I'd heard many times, sometimes speaking to me in intuitive flashes, but more often, when I wrote in my journal, it flowed as a stream of ideas emerging from an awareness much deeper than my conscious mind. Whenever I felt this flow of inspiration, I relaxed, listened, felt joy, and welcomed the guidance from my Higher Self. It was a motivating presence that had been with me since my origins as a young girl living with my family in New York City. I had been raised with no religion, no metaphysics, no idea of any kind of greater existence, and so this inner voice became the agent of transformation in my life.

While I had no idea of this then, I know now that all of us have this inner voice. It is the Higher Self, the Essential Self, within each of us—which *is* each of us—and it is communicating with us all the time. Sometimes we hear it, and sometimes we don't, but it is never really silent.

My experience with this beloved inner voice deepened through the years, so I decided to expand my experience of it by formally pursuing what is now called the Emergence Process. Each day I create my own Inner Sanctuary, both internally and as a physical space. I go to my writing table and simply allow the inner voice to write.

Remember, the inner voice is present in each of us as our own Essential Self. Through the Emergence Process, we access the Self and begin the lifelong process of incarnating that essence. This is a life practice I do every morning, and I recommend that you try it too, as it is a fundamental practice in the Hub of the Wheel.

I am so excited about the thought of us doing this together on a global scale. It could actually be a vital factor in making the Shift in time. The Emergence Process provides us with an early developmental path to our own birthing as Universal Humans. The inner shifting is vital for the outer shifting. A spiritual, developmental path toward our emergence as co-creators is vital and designed precisely for this moment of the Planetary Shift. To catalyze your emergence, my familial sister Patricia Ellsberg and I have developed an online course called Emergence: The Shift from Ego to Essence. She and I invite you to join us so we can cocreate a tide of inner shifting together! In addition, a guide to use to further your emergence practice is provided in my book *Emergence: The Shift from Ego to Essence* (revised 2012 edition).[5]

Another fundamental practice to sustain inner shifting can also be found in my book *52 Codes for Conscious Self Evolution*.[6]

2. Cultivating Heart Coherence in the Hub

The Hub becomes the ultimate gathering place of all those

who are "in action" for the Birth; supporting it are what spiritual author Eckhart Tolle terms "frequency holders." Their function is to anchor the frequency of the cocreative consciousness on this planet. Whenever we are in the Hub, we can feel the frequencies of the Field, the presence of the noosphere. In their essays, Welcoming Committee member Lynne McTaggart call this place "the bond," and Ashok Gangadean names it "((Presence))." Following the lead of the Institute of HearthMath, I prefer to call it global heart coherence, a phrase based in the most recent scientific research.

How do we achieve heart coherence at the global level? To understand this, imagine that within the Hub is what might be called a "still center." This space is the global Field into which religious and spiritual groups of all kinds across the globe continually contribute the energetics of their meditation, stillness, prayer, and worship. In our preferred terminology, we are cultivating *global coherence* when we engage in any such heart-based spiritual practice; we are moving from ego to essence and identifying with our Essential Self and its energies.

The word "coherence" refers to the creative heart impulse in each of us that is connecting with the same impulse in others around the world. This field of coherence and love is a vital contribution to gentling the Birth toward the next stage of our evolution. The principle of heart coherence is described by Claudia Welss in detail in the "Special Essays" section in Part IV of this book. Welss is a director for both the Foundation for Conscious Evolution and also for the Global Coherence Initiative at the Institute of HeartMath. In the essay she states:

> In *The Powers of the Universe*, cosmologist Brian Swimme states, "Life has a new demand on us—the demand of synergy through conscious self-awareness." Our hypothesis, based on my work at the nexus of *heart coherence* and social synergy, is that the "demand of synergy" can be met through an attention to

heart coherence—and that a state of "inner synergy" is a necessary condition for the successful expression of "outer synergy" in social systems. Heart coherence enables inner synergy by creating the physiological conditions for its emergence. It allows us to *embody synergy*, and in so doing, to become architects of global change by cocreating the energetic field conditions under which social synergy is more likely to emerge. In other words, in the Hub of the Wheel we use our own resonance . . . to energize the natural forces of attraction and connectivity to "turn the Wheel."

Claudia goes on to explain how the act of generating energetic coherence is essential for a whole-system shift:

Incoherence creates separation and obstructs communication at all levels. When information exchange is constrained, a system can fall into disequilibrium. We can predict the influence of human incoherence and the resulting disequilibrium on the social systems arising from such conditions. Attention to the *energetic design* underlying our attempts at synergy seems as important, then, as attention to the *social design*. In fact, the success of the social architecture seems reliant on the quality of the energetic architecture from which it arises. The Hub, the Wheel of Cocreation, Shift Circles, and Syncons are all social design innovations intended to help us "jump the Gap." But we also need to consciously design environments capable of supporting them. Without our conscious attention, it is our unconscious that in-forms this field by default. While the *capacity* for expressing coherence is innate, conscious proficiency in setting this capacity in motion is an inner technology that satisfies the Hub function of creating a coherent field that enables synergistic convergence.

For these reasons and others I advocate using HeartMath techniques for creating heart coherence and resonance within the Hub. In particular, I recommend that everyone use the Institute of HeartMath's *Quick Coherence*™ and *Heart Lock-In*™ practices, which are based on over thirty years of scientific research on the psychophysiology of heart coherence. (I also urge those who are so inclined to enter the Global Birthing Care Room, explained below.)

We only have space here to present a brief overview of HeartMath practices written with the assistance of Claudia Welss and the Institute of HeartMath. Please refer to the Institute's website for more information on processes, research studies, and supportive tools.

Quick Coherence: This important practice is comprised of three simple steps:

The first step is *heart-focus*. Shift your attention to the area of your heart, putting your hand over your heart if that helps. Notice if the rhythm of your breathing changes with this shift of attention. You may sense a perceptual shift, as though you're perceiving through your heart instead of only through your brain.

The next step while maintaining heart-focus is *heart-breathing*. Imagine your breath flowing in and out through your heart, letting your breath rather than your mind direct the flow. Allow your breathing to be a little longer and a little deeper than normal but still casual and comfortable. Use your breathing to help you let go of any resistance you're having. As you focus your attention on the heart in this way, your breath and your attention start to *resonate* in the heart. This can feel relaxing, as if you are moving into a more neutral state. You may feel your concerns begin to melt away. Just keep imagining your breath flowing in and out through the heart. (Again, while this practice can be relaxing, heart coherence is an active state; it should be distinguished from relaxation, which requires only a lowered heart rate and not necessarily a coherent rhythm.)

Next, maintain heart-focus and heart-breathing as we engage the third and most important step, which is *heart-feeling*. This is not simple cheerfulness; it's more like an inner smile that evokes feelings of appreciation or love—such as those you may have for a special person, a pet, something in nature, or even for God or humanity. Try not to stay with the thought that evokes the feeling; let ideas or images drop away. Experience *the feeling*. If you have trouble experiencing such a feeling, simply hold an attitude instead of an idea—of appreciation, care, gratitude, or compassion, or any other sincere positive attitude. Once you've shifted to a positive feeling or attitude, sustain it by continuing heart-focus, heart-breathing, and heart-feeling. It's the sustained *sincere* feeling or attitude that anchors the physiological changes and creates the dramatic shift into heart coherence.

Heart Lock-In: Continue on after the Quick Coherence practice by allowing the sustained feeling to expand through your body, and sending that feeling of love, care, or appreciation to people in your life. Imagine including people you don't know but who are participating in Birth 2012 with you. Imagine coherent waveforms radiating out into the world; then imagine experiencing the heart coherence transmitted by others. By intentionally radiating coherent heart energy through the heart's electromagnetic field we may even imagine charging the noosphere, magnifying its coherence.

The Global Birthing Care Room: Quick Coherence and Heart Lock-In can now be practiced in a special group setting online. The Global Birthing Care Room, a project of the Institute for HeartMath's Global Coherence Initiative, provides a digital representation of practitioners, portraying them as points of light across the globe.[7]

As we enter this online space in increasing numbers and as our most heart-coherent selves, we can visualize that we are imprinting the noosphere with an increasingly coherent pattern. As microcosms of the Shift ourselves, we can recognize that in every moment we are contributing energetic patterns that either add to or diminish the field of global resonance. In the Hub of the Wheel, as digitally mirrored in the space of the Care Room, we commit to moving beyond feeling the presence of the Field to actually in-forming it with our own coherence. With a critical mass of "small islands of coherence," we may even facilitate a shift to the next phase of evolution.

Of course, nobody fully knows all the energetic factors that will facilitate the Planetary Shift. But it has been suggested by HeartMath that if approximately three hundred and fifty thousand of us are in a state of heart coherence together, this could provide the baseline of coherence required to significantly advance the birthing process. Creating heart coherence is an effective contribution that we can all act on now.[8]

3. Creating Synergy in the Hub through Evolutionary Shift Circles

The design of what we call Evolutionary Shift Circles (or Shift Circles for short) is crucial to the energetic architecture of the Shift. Of the many kinds of spiritual circles in the world, Evolutionary Shift Circles are especially designed for those of us who seek to work together for the Planetary Birth. If you desire to form one, we suggest you and your group consider these core Shift Circle Agreements:

- Set a firm intention and fully commit to being part of the Planetary Shift.

- Engage in practices that create a feeling of love and heart connection with each other.

- Actively give your gifts to the Shift—create forms of shared service with others in your Shift Circle.

Shift Circles have been forming all over the world for several years. And when they align around the shared purpose of awakening a critical mass of coherence on December 22, 2012, they will be vital agents to gentle the Birth.

The most comprehensive overview on how to form Shift Circles can be found in *The Co-Creator's Handbook* by Carolyn Anderson (with Katharine Roske). This book is based upon our shared experience in the formation of Circles, including my experience of forming "Positive Future Centers" as described in the next chapter.[9]

Of course, you may use any one of a variety of Circle methods that resonate with the needs of those you are "hubbing" with. Literally hundreds of methods and techniques now exist, but the technique that I especially recommend now is called the Vistar Method.

The Vistar Method: This approach evolved over sixteen years of committed, cutting-edge work on convening Circles, and I believe it is uniquely suited for collective evolutionary awakening in support of the Birth.

The Vistar Method provides four guidelines and a simple structure. The guidelines, called GuideRules, are deeply rooted in metaphysical principles that are easy to apply. The Vistar GuideRules address the focusing of attention and energy in a group so that the whole can move to new levels of understanding, connection, and meaning. The Method's disciplined format allows transformative meetings where individuals can break through barriers to authenticity and work together synergistically. The creators of Vistar, Ron Friedman, MD, and Victoria Friedman, also point to a less tangible factor, "the magic of conscious partnership with the Creative Source, which can uplift and infuse gatherings with a sense of unity and meaning and a vision of purpose. It's about energy, clarity, and moving beyond the quagmires and barriers experienced in normal group communication in evolutionary groups, businesses, in families, and certainly on the world stage."

The Vistar Method is easy to learn and can be used for a small or large number of participants. It defines three roles for each meeting: the Leader, the Support, and the Participant, each with their own responsibility to the Circle.

I have found that, as the frequency of such meetings increases, a direct heartfelt experience of connectedness emerges within the group for immense new possibilities. The Vistar Method is both an art form and a cocreative social structure, and a good way to get started when creating a Shift Circle.[10]

4. Activating Our Vocational Arousal

Essence is creative. No matter what our current work, profession, or job, unrealized creativity exists in every one of us. As we increasingly merge with our Essential Selves, it is natural for our unique creativity to rise to the surface. One result is that we become energized to seek for our true life purpose. This search can lead to the marvelous excitement of "vocational arousal," which I earlier discussed in detail with Jan Phillips. We can also become vocationally aroused within the Field of coherence and love that gets created in Shift Circles and through other Hub activities.

We've seen that when we experience vocational arousal, our sexual drive for union with another expands into what I call the "suprasexual drive." This shift is a bio-evolutionary phenomenon in which the natural urge to *procreate* emerges in a new form as our heart's desire to *cocreate*. Deep down, we all yearn to discover not only our real life callings but also our true partners in our lifework.

So, in the Hub of the Wheel, we need processes and practices that actually help us discover and nurture such vocations of destiny, and that help us to find partners and teammates with whom to cocreate. You can learn much more about this phenomenon of vocational arousal in my book coauthored with Marion Head, entitled *Suprasexual rEvolution: A Radical Path to 2012 and Beyond.* [11]

As we will see in the next chapter, these evolutionary Hub practices are essential to the ever-evolving work of the inner and outer shift. Engaging with the twelve sectors in the Wheel of Cocreation, as well as with its several rings, can now become the locus for the expression of the social synergy needed for the Planetary Birth.

Chapter 5

Creating Social Synergy

We have entered the Hub of the Wheel, and are learning to become cocreators of the Shift through a variety of processes and practices, personally and in small core groups. But we still face the larger question: Will humanity be able to act in time to tip the scales in favor of a positive future at the *global* level, given the rapid escalation of problems that threaten our survival?

Ironically, as planetary conditions become more chaotic, the prospects for positive change actually become better. As we have noted, evolution is able to adapt by repatterning itself quickly during times of extreme instability. And it is here that we can find a scientific basis for our potential to "cross the gap."

We earlier discussed how at each crossroads in biological evolution, the immediate crisis of survival faced by a species or an ecosystem is what drives its processes of adaptation. Indeed, the threats we currently face are catalyzing millions of us to engage in personal transformative processes such as those we have just presented. These practices are a crucial part of the urgent work of the repatterning of human society. But they are just a prelude to the path of *social* transformation that we will examine in this chapter. Crucial innovations in all sectors of society, plus a variety of new methods of social synergy, will soon reveal a powerful *collective* path of repatterning.

In order to deepen our understanding of such a profound evolutionary process, let us return to the basic science—which in part arises from the application of complexity theory to biology—and ask this question: How does nature's capacity to take unexpected "quantum jumps" apply to us in our current situation?

How a Living System Cooperates in Its Own Self-Transcendence

I had been searching for years to find the missing link that could help us get across the gap, when I discovered a vital clue in the *New York Times* in 1977. It was a story about the chemist and Nobel Prize–winner, Ilya Prigogine (pronounced *prig-a-gene*). He had discovered the process whereby life evolves into more complex systems even in the face of the second law of thermodynamics, which states that in a closed system energy inevitably increases in entropy or disorder. We saw earlier that, based on this "fatal" law, scientists predicted that the universe would inevitably end in a "heat death"— the degradation of all energy in the universe to a state of inert uniformity. We noted how this law formed the scientific basis of much of modern pessimism.

How, then, in the face of this inevitable tendency for the universe to increase in disorder, has more complex order increased for billions of years? What are the mechanisms whereby higher order is achieved in nature? And how might we learn from this process to facilitate our own leap to higher order?

The answer seems to lay in Prigogine's theory of dissipative structures. A dissipative structure is any living system in nature whose form or structure is maintained by a continuous consumption of energy—known in physics as "dissipation." All living systems are dissipative structures—including humans. In a real sense, living things have been running uphill in a universe that is supposed to be running down!

Here's how it works: The continuous movement of energy through the system results in fluctuations, which, if minor, do not alter its structural integrity. But if the fluctuations reach a critical size, they perturb the system. They increase the number of novel interactions within it. The elements of the old pattern come into contact with each other in *new* ways and make *new* connections. The parts reorganize into a new whole—and the system "escapes" into a higher order! In other words, life has the potential to create new forms by allowing a shake-up of old forms. Prigogine showed that the elements of a dissipative structure cooperate to bring about this transformation of the whole.

When I read this, I immediately realized how society could make a quantum jump from our current crises to a future that is equal to our new powers. Back in 1977, I could already see that we would never get there by linear, incremental steps alone, given the world's accumulating crises; all the more so now. But thankfully, the process of transformation is not linear! Systems become more complex by nonlinear processes, exponentially increasing the numbers of interactions of incremental innovations.

At some point, apparently insignificant innovations connect in a nonlinear manner. As Teilhard de Chardin might put it, everything that rises converges and connects, becomes synergistic and cocreative. The system then cooperates in its own self-transcendence in an apparent sudden shift. This shift has been building for a long time and born out of myriad innovations silently and invisibly interacting and connecting beneath the surface of our attention.

Let's apply the Prigogine model to our personal and social evolution. If nature has been working through dissipative structures for billions of years, the same process must be working through us now. Let us enter the Hub of the Wheel of Cocreation and find out!

Today our global civilization is a large dissipative structure increasingly perturbed and undergoing fluctuations, and throughout the world, systems are increasingly unstable or dysfunctional. We are using more of our energy to handle these problems but in ways that seem ineffective—like building more and more weapons and prisons for greater security or fighting a war against drugs when kids roam aimlessly in the streets with nothing to do and nowhere to go. Hunger, poverty, social and economic injustice, global warming, resource depletion, pollution, overpopulation, the loss of rain forests—all these factors are escalating and are now tending to converge in catastrophe. The essay contribution in this book by Ervin Laszlo, one of our Welcoming Committee members, lists these challenges in detail.

At the same time, innovations of all kinds in all fields, or "new mutations," are springing up everywhere. Thousands of acts of caring, sharing, and healing, as well as new social and political solutions are emerging. Applying the model of dissipative structures to our situation, we see that—while threats are accumulating that are destabilizing the system— social innovations that share a similar value system are also converging, connecting, and networking at an increasing rate. And this process is accelerating rapidly with the help of the Internet.

But will the convergence of positive innovations happen before the convergence of destructive tendencies? Will the planetary system repattern to a higher order, or will it fall apart into the political chaos and environmental collapse that has been predicted? This, of course, is the great question. There is no guarantee that a dissipative structure will repattern to a higher order. It is merely a tendency, just as it is the tendency of each baby to survive its birth, although many do not.

It is precisely at this point that we need a new social innovation to facilitate the increased interaction among the positive innovations—a fresh articulation of the whole to facilitate the convergence. And this is the purpose of introducing the Wheel of Cocreation. As it turns, we can set in motion a new social function to hasten the nonlinear interaction of positive innovations and thereby facilitate the natural repatterning of our society to a more harmonious order, thus saving ourselves from predicted catastrophes. Joseph Chilton Pearce put it this way in his 2002 book, *The Crack in the Cosmic Egg*:

> A system in balance and functioning well is difficult to change, but as a system falls into disorder, change becomes more and more feasible and finally inevitable. At that inevitable point the least bit of coherent order can bring to order the whole disorderly array. Which direction the change takes depends on the nature of the chaotic attractor that lifts the chaos into its new order. If that chaotic attractor is demonic, the old cycle simply repeats itself, which seems to have been historically the case for our species. But if the chaotic attractor were benevolent or "divine," the new order would have to be of that same nature.

My 1984 Electoral Campaign for a Positive Future

After I discovered this clue of how nature evolves with the help of the Prigogine model, I wanted to find a way to test my discovery in the real world. In 1984, I decided to do an experiment in conscious evolution by bringing the ideas of Prigogine, Abraham Maslow, Teilhard de Chardin, Buckminster Fuller, and many other new-paradigm thinkers into the political arena. I became an "idea candidate" for the future of humanity, offering a method to accelerate the interaction of positive innovations and help the system repattern itself in the midst of its crisis.

After a great deal of consultation with others, I formed the Campaign for a Positive Future. I told all my friends and colleagues that I was in the running for selection as the Democratic vice-presidential candidate by whomever was nominated for president. I asked them to arrange opportunities for me to speak in order to gain support for my ideas. Many were delighted. Meetings were arranged, and I set out upon the most fascinating journey of my life.

This video tells the full story of Barbara's 1984 vice-presidential campaign.

To launch the campaign, I created a new social function called the Office for the Future, or Peace Room, whose purpose would be that of converging crucial innovations at the highest level of power. It was to reside in the office of the vice president of the United States, and in its design this office would become as sophisticated as a war room. In our war rooms we track enemies and strategize on how to defeat them; by contrast, the Peace Room would identify, connect, and communicate our successes and models that work. I proposed that the Office for the Future should have four functions that would facilitate the repatterning of our society to a higher order of consciousness, freedom, and synergistic order:

1. The office would scan for breakthroughs in all fields—health, education, media, science, government, business, the arts, and community. It would also invite citizens at the local level to form centers to scan their communities for creative innovations; our foreign ambassadors would even be asked to establish Peace Rooms in their countries.

2. The office would map these innovations according to sector and geography to discover the pattern and design of what works. We envisioned large maps and graphs in the White House that would show progress toward the evolutionary agenda—the hierarchy of social needs—with constant input based on what innovators are doing that works.

    As part of the official United States Bicentennial celebration in 1976, I organized a Syncon, a successful conference for "synergistic convergence," in Washington, DC. This early version of a Peace Room had a similar goal: We graphically presented a social-needs hierarchy. From all over the country, people called in with their social innovations, which were placed on the chart. The conference participants came to understand how a new social system was evolving in a coherent way. (I discuss the phenomenon of Syncons later in this chapter.)

3. The office would help social innovators make vital and necessary connections with others. When we find our teammates and partners, the deep human desire to relate, to connect, to join our

genius is satisfied. Cocreation does not mean service at the sacrifice of Self; it means service through the actualization of Self. Self-actualization occurs when we find our vocations and express them meaningfully in the world. Our vocations are drawn forth by the process of finding others we need to work with, by enlivening our individual lives and the quality of life in our communities.

4. The office would communicate via all levels of media the stories of the human family's successes and model projects. I suggested there be a weekly broadcast from the White House—What Works in America— calling for greater public participation, inviting people to join projects, to start new ones, to find their life purpose, and to come together to create the works and acts needed for the future of the human family. Volunteerism would come alive as the expression of our love and creativity in chosen work.

Positive Future Centers Spring Up

With this proposal, I sent out a "high fidelity bird call," as economist Hazel Henderson put it, and I got a certain kind of bird. It was thrilling. Everywhere I went people said they wanted to form a center for "it"—whatever *it* was! We were not quite a political philosophy or a new party; I came to realize that "it" was the creative essence in each person awakened, amplified, and manifested in cocreative action. People sought communion and community, not something that any leader could do for them. Yet they found it exciting to have a political candidate support them in their initiatives.

One of the most amazing aspects of my campaign is that little centers spontaneously sprung up everywhere, calling themselves Positive Future Centers. They were actually embryonic centers for cocreation in the Hub of the Wheel. In these centers, people meditated and prayed; they worked on themselves and they reached into their communities, making contributions by expressing their life purpose.

Wherever I went during the campaign, I was at home. Each center was resonant with the evolutionary agenda and affirmed the new paradigm. People were interested in both human and social potential. They were eager to carry their inner work into the world. Our goal was to model the change we wanted to see in the world. "The best solution is our own conscious evolution," was one of our slogans.

As the weeks and months passed, the time finally came to attend the Democratic National Convention. Politically sophisticated people told me, "Don't go to San Francisco, dear. You have done a good job at the grassroots level, but they will destroy you at a national convention." We had no money left, no media attention (we were told we were "too positive"!), and no passes to the floor (the Democratic National Committee had ignored our campaign entirely).

However impossible it seemed from any rational logic, ten of us decided to go to the convention; my guidance was clear that we had not yet completed our mission. My purpose had been to speak at the convention and call for the Office for the Future and the Peace Room. I was to tell the story of humanity's evolutionary potential in a political context and plant the idea of the evolutionary agenda as an approach to politics that focused on *what works.*

Our task was to have two hundred delegates sign a petition that would place my name in nomination; this would make me eligible to make my nominating speech before the convention, the nation, and the world. We were racked with doubt, for I had enough sense as a political science graduate to know that this goal was

impossible. I should give up before suffering the hu-
miliation of being totally ignored, for the chances of a
grassroots, futuristic, unknown woman being nominated
for the vice presidency of the United States was less than
zero. I was told we would be lucky to get one delegate,
even if she were my mother!

We decided, however, to act as if we were going to
succeed and to practice every metaphysical discipline any
of us had learned. We arose at five every morning. We
prayed; we loved one another; we forgave one another;
we did creative visualizations of the nominating speech;
we affirmed our victory with certainty.

As the proceedings opened, we went into the hallways,
the bars, the restaurants, and the early morning caucuses to sign up delegates. Occasionally I was given thirty
seconds to speak at the caucuses. I was able to say, "My
name is Barbara Marx Hubbard, I am running for the vice
presidency to propose an Office for the Future that will
scan for, map, connect, and communicate positive innovations that work." And the delegates signed up. My team
of ten people—only one of whom had ever been to a national convention—obtained most of the signatures. The
resonance we had created among ourselves radiated and
seemed to mesmerize the busy delegates. Still, the odds
were against us; many powerful political leaders were vy-
ing for this nomination, for it meant a televised speech
before the world. We were up against a substantial field of
well-known political leaders who were also attempting to
obtain the two hundred required signatures.

The first day we had one hundred signatures. The second day we had another hundred. On the third day, my
campaign manager, Faye Beuby, took the petitions to the
Democratic National Committee at the convention. We
had more than two hundred valid signatures. The Committee was horrified! Someone had gotten through the
net. Then the announcement came: two women's names
were to be placed in nomination for the vice presidency

of the United States: Barbara Marx Hubbard and Geraldine Ferraro. I was stunned. It was a political paranormal experience! The impossible had happened! Social synergy had won the day!

A few days later, when I was taken to the huge dais to speak to the convention, a guard led me to the microphone, holding my arm gently. "Honey," he said, "don't worry, they won't pay any attention to you, they never do . . . you're saying this for the universe." And so I did. I said, "The purpose of the United States of America is to emancipate the creativity of people everywhere."

With all the power of my being I called for a new social function, the Peace Room, in the White House. The delegates were milling around, paying no attention, but as I spoke the words I realized for the first time the enormous power of focused action and faith. If a disorganized band of grassroots environmentalists, businesspeople, housewives, futurists, and human potentialists could achieve this, imagine what we could do if we were well organized!

Today we *have* this ability to get organized, and of course a key vehicle is the Birth 2012 campaign itself, plus the global movement it will catalyze with the help of The Shift Network, the Welcoming Committee, and *you*. In 1984, ninety Positive Future Centers arose overnight in the United States; and now, a generation later, Shift Circles are being formed worldwide, inspired by this possibility of the Great Shift. Later in this chapter we will learn more about how Circles can lead to larger-scale opportunities for participation.

Enjoy this historic footage of Barbara's speech to the 1984 Democratic Convention.

Activating the Wheel of Cocreation

We've noted that the Core of the Spiral is now breaking through in millions of us, whereas in earlier stages of evolution it only entered into the consciousness of a few, extraordinary individuals. It is showing up in the commitments of today's evolutionary leaders who embrace conscious evolution; it is also expressed "on the streets" in the political and cultural ferment that we see now throughout the world. Indeed, these pioneering souls who are now working for systemic change are becoming the "new norm."

The Wheel of Cocreation is a potent representation of the whole-system shift. If you look carefully into the Wheel you will see twelve societal sectors arranged in a wheel-like structure according to the so-called "12 around 1" model; we believe these twelve areas comprise the full list of the basic functions of any community. The "12 around 1" principle is considered to be a model of stability in nature, and is the basis of the concept of "tensegrity" pioneered by Buckminster Fuller. Thus, the sectors or functions represented by the Wheel provide us with a reliable and integrative model for our collective transformation—twelve divisions of the positive fluctuations needed to create a leap to social synergy. With these same principles in mind, we also have invited *twelve* individuals to become the Welcoming Committee for Birth 2012.

It is our responsibility now to activate the Wheel of Cocreation—our turn on the Spiral. From the point of view of evolution, the Wheel represents a vital step forward toward a cooperative world. But the Wheel is not initially a model of government; instead, it points to a holistic, grassroots process that facilitates synergy, where we seek common goals and match needs and resources throughout the whole system, rather than remain isolated in disconnected pursuits.

When you have discovered your vocation of destiny through evolutionary Hub practices and activities and by personal discernment, you are ready to enter the Wheel with your creative project. Practically speaking, your work will relate to some field, enterprise, or endeavor within society, such as health, education, economics, environment, justice, governance, science, the arts, or media, as shown in detail in Figure 2.

Your crucial work is to place your desire to express your vocation in that sector of the Wheel to which you are most called. There you will find others who may be the partners you are looking for. You can now enter a dynamic evolutionary process in which you unite with others around what you want to create, and connect with those who need what you have to give. Your sector becomes a place to experience vocational arousal, to form vocational cores, and to manifest creative projects and initiatives of all kinds. There are also guides and leaders in every sector of the Wheel to inspire and inform you.

Remember that in the Wheel, we are fostering a more cocreative society and a more participatory, synergistic democracy—not by revolution but by evolutionary action.

Please have a look below at Figure 2: The Wheel of Cocreation.

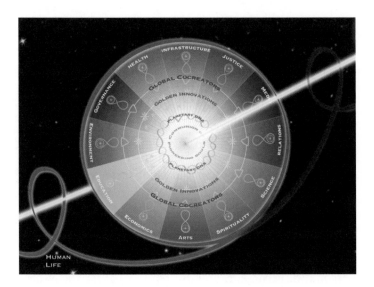

*Figure 2: The Wheel of Cocreation. A high-resolution version of
this image can be found at Birth2012.com.*

The Wheel, just like my Peace Room model, serves
as a new function of social synergy with which to continually scan for, map, connect, and communicate what
is working in the world. At first it is simply a symbolic
vehicle of our creative action. But, hopefully, it may one
day become an institutional force in the way it was intended in my vice-presidential campaign.

When the Wheel of Cocreation is fully activated,
we will see the new world that is already arising in our
midst. It will offer us a coherent picture of humanity as
well as our whole planetary system as a living organism.
It will tell us where the problems are, who is working to
solve them, and where we can find the needed innovations—all organic elements of a living, holistic system of
relationships. It will provide for us what I call the *new
news* of who we are becoming in such a way as to continually activate our potential to participate.

Fostering Social Synergy through the Wheel

Imagine that the Wheel is "coming alive"! It has become a magnetic matrix attracting into itself *what is working*. As people and projects enter the Wheel, they place their work in clusters based on similar functions. Every sector is connected to every other sector. The purpose is to enable us to make as many connections as possible across sectors.

Let's imagine that you have already placed yourself in the sector of the Wheel where you feel your primary call and you have found others who share that passion. It's now time to reach out to people who are involved in other sectors vital to fulfilling your purpose. Notice the aspects of your goal that connect with other parts in the Wheel and dive deeply into those connections.

As the Wheel turns, it pulls everyone forward. It takes us across the evolutionary gap from *Here*, our current state of overpopulation, pollution, resource depletion, war, etc., to *There*, an ever evolving, sustainable, compassionate, and cocreative world. Remember that the turning Wheel is nonlinear. Our objective is not incremental, linear change. It's too late for that. Our goal is to cocreate small islands of coherence in the sea of social chaos. By consciously creating such "fluctuations" in the system, we emulate the way in which nature takes quantum jumps through greater synergy. Novel elements come together, making rapid connections in order to form a new whole that is both unpredictable and greater than the sum of its parts. The resulting "mutant" system is something radically new.

In a kind of biomimicry, or what might be called "evomimicry"—a beautiful term coined by Claudia Welss— we are imitating the evolutionary tendency of nature to form new systems out of new parts; and our method now is to do this *consciously*, as people link up with each other and connect the projects that are working. The

Internet alone is permitting this to happen with much greater facility than the Campaign for a Positive Future could ever have done in 1984!

Indeed, we may well be at the threshold of a non-linear exponential interaction of innovating elements—a convergence powerful enough that our crises-ridden social system can cooperate in its own self-transcendence. This would be social synergy at its best—the exponential interaction and communication of that which is already working to heal and evolve our world.

Thus, the most important social purpose for each of us right now is to facilitate the connectivity of the "islands" of what really *works*. I call those who are devoted to this vital purpose the Global Communion of Pioneering Souls, the first ring beyond the Hub of the Wheel. Remember, what makes all this possible is the fact that nature's tendency to self-organize into more synergistic systems is happening *within* us now, animated by the Impulse of Evolution that runs through the Wheel of Cocreation.

The Global Communion of Pioneering Souls

When we resonate and participate with others in the Hub of the Wheel, we also can visualize and feel that we are members of the Global Communion—people everywhere on Earth, from every culture, race, faith, age, color, and background who feel within ourselves the rising tide of Spirit, our yearning to give our greater gift, our heart's desire to participate in some way in a better world for our children and all Earth life. This communion is now awakening all over the world because it is "planetary time" for a quantum social leap.

Earth has given birth to bacteria, to cells, to animals, to self-conscious humans, and now to a new life form—the Universal Human. My sense is that there are enough of us to shift the world—provided we are *connected*. In the last chapter, I listed some recommended ways to do so, including connecting in Evolutionary Shift Circles through heart coherence, the Vistar Method, and vocational arousal. And now we can do so by engaging in sectors of the Wheel through methods of social synergy.

All of us attracted to this positive shift are natural members of the Communion of Pioneering Souls. We are already self-assembling for the birthing process. The networks in health, education, energy, new media, and emerging forms of conscious business are already taking shape. And we are now beginning to *network the networks* of positive change. And just as the breakdowns can go quantum, so can breakthroughs be accelerated.

We are right on the threshold of the Great Shift now. Think of all the people you know and love who are doing some good in the world. Reach out in your heart and touch them now. Appreciate them. Connect with them. Imagine how many people they know who are also awakening and who are also connecting. Imagine all of this connecting and converging, as a vital expression of our Planetary Shift. I call this is an experience of evolutionary communion. My *Evolutionary Communion* guidebook offers a text and CD concerning the nature and functions of the Evolutionary Communion of Pioneering Souls.[12]

As we symbolically step out of the Hub of the Wheel to the ring beyond the Pioneering Souls, we next see a small double helix-like line called the Planetary DNA. This signifies the discovery of the metapattern of the emerging world; the evolutionary design or structure through which we can move to higher order. The Planetary DNA, or metapattern, is continually being discovered by identifying projects that are working already. We are calling these Golden Innovations.

Golden Innovations That Work

The Hub of the Wheel has an integral relationship to the twelve sectors. Recall that the Hub is a sacred space in our consciousness—an incredibly fertile domain. At a personal level, it is a place in consciousness where we can deepen our evolutionary capacities as we shift from ego to essence and more fully access our vocations of destiny. Energetically, it is a place where we resonate with one another to create global heart coherence—an important practice essential to social synergy. Socially and culturally, it is the space where we will discover the patterns of a cocreative society. And with evolutionary eyes, we can see it as a place where new design innovations pertaining to every sector of the Wheel are now breaking through into awareness. In other words, the Hub is an "evolutionary design space"—the same space out of which nature has evolved designs like galaxies, starfish, and photosynthesis. Of course, in our case, the design work in each sector of the Wheel is conscious, creative, and contributing to the Planetary Shift.

Imagine the Hub and the Global Communion of Pioneering Souls surrounded by the great innovators and visionary creators of our time, those who have already learned how to make the world work through some vital and practical endeavor. This ring will include Welcoming Committee members such as Rinaldo Brutoco in economics, James O'Dea in peacebuilding, Michael Beckwith and Oscar Miro-Quesada in spirituality, and Jean Houston in arts and creativity. As a member of the Communion of Pioneering Souls, you can observe these creators and innovators acting as stewards, initiators, and luminaries within every sector of the Wheel. Notice also that people from all walks of life are being attracted to their new functions and life purpose within the Wheel. See them entering every sector, experiencing vocational arousal and finding their teammates, telling their stories as the *new* news, and connecting and learning from the growing community of cocreators worldwide.

This emergent community of pioneers is consciously motivated by the Impulse of Evolution, and as a result, new design concepts constantly emerge; indeed, the cream of these designs—or Golden Innovations—are being gathered in each sector of the Wheel. A Golden Innovation is a project now working successfully that, if further developed and applied, could transform the system in which it functions. It differs from a simply good innovation in that it could have a systemic effect in addressing a major social ill. Some of our Welcoming Committee members have already achieved that status in their work, but there are hundreds more of such radical innovations scattered across the social body that are not yet connected—not yet synergized with the whole.

In the sectors of the Wheel, you see Golden Innovations that work. Each sector is designed to be filled with successful projects and innovations. They are already revealing to us the design and pattern of the emerging world.

Each innovation to be placed in the Wheel follows certain basic values, such as nonviolence, sustainability, equality, cooperation, and cocreativity. And they should always reflect the ultimate evolutionary value of moving us toward higher consciousness and greater freedom through more complex or synergistic order. Any act, intention, or belief that expands our consciousness toward a more unitive, spiritual, loving, and whole-centered stage is favored. Innovations that lead to greater freedom and responsibility are selected— freedom *from* deficiencies of hunger, poverty, lack of self-esteem, and freedom *to* realize our untapped potential for self-actualization and chosen life purpose. Acts that value synergistic ("win-win-win") order, or that help bring separate parts together into greater wholeness and cooperation are also favored. Remember that nature selects for what cooperates best.

The Wheel is a context for "mini-memes," ideas that hold the seed of the emerging civilization. As genes build bodies, memes build cultures. We can envision, as this process continues, that every sector of the Wheel will fill with many projects that work, memes of social, spiritual, scientific, and technological innovations that foster sustainability, compassion, spiritual fulfillment, and innovations that liberate and transform. Eventually we will discover the memetic code of a cocreative society based on the interconnectivity of projects actually working to heal and evolve our world.

In my book *Conscious Evolution: Awakening the Power of our Social Potential*,[13] I quote Eleanor LeCain, who helps us define Golden Innovations in a practical sense: "They are projects now working successfully that, if further developed and applied, could have a quantum effect in addressing a major social ill or realizing a new possibility. Golden Innovations are mutually reinforcing and interconnecting. They foster intrinsic values by embodying greater cooperation, creativity, optimism, governance for differences, a sense of reverence for life, and faith in the potential of all people. They emphasize self-actualization rather than self-sacrifice. They assist in the evolution of a vital function in the social body. They are more cost-effective and sustainable. They do not depend on one charismatic leader alone."

As Golden Innovations are placed in every sector of the Wheel, we make visible the key features of the approaching era of conscious evolution. This is one of the great functions of the Wheel of Cocreation: connecting the dots of what is already working now. This rapid connectivity among the best projects and memes is a crucial mission of the Birth 2012 movement, and I strongly suggest that you access our special website devoted to this purpose, Birth2012.com. I believe this collaborative work can foster an uprising of creativity, hope, and genius that will transform the world!

Global Cocreators

Surrounding the part of the Wheel called Golden Innovations is a circle called Global Cocreators, made up of remarkable and successful innovators in every field. We know many of them. They exist in every community as gifted initiators of improved economic systems, health practices, energy systems, modes of cooperative leadership and management, and more. One of the functions of Pioneering Souls in every community is to *identify* Global Cocreators, to call them into our Circles and Town Meetings in the Round (which are explained below), thereby drawing on the existing genius of our communities. They are already present in society, but often are not recognized or invited to be included in local movements. Good examples of Global Cocreators that I have identified are found in *Visions of a Universal Humanity*, the second DVD in my Humanity Ascending documentary series.[14]

Building Evolutionary Community

As a communicator of conscious evolution, I have been yearning for many years to be part of a greater community of pioneering souls, both globally and locally. Like me, most of us who are attracted to cocreating our future beyond the Birth feel somewhat alone. True, we are emerging everywhere as pioneers and cocreators, but often we are not connected to each other locally in groups, and usually we do not belong to a larger community other than in an online setting. Yet I feel certain that building evolutionary local communities is essential. In fact, it is one of the most important acts of our time! We simply cannot do this work alone. That is why I strongly encourage everyone, at a minimum, to meet regularly face-to-face with a few pioneers in an Evolutionary Shift Circle.

But we also need to design more extended community beyond meeting in Circles. Toward that goal, I am so delighted to be working with my evolutionary team, especially Judy Cauley and Patricia Gaul, to develop processes and practices that will assist us in stabilizing evolutionary awareness in local communities. In response to this basic need, Judy, Patricia, and I are creating a new evolutionary learning path to awaken, deepen, and *live* the ideals of conscious evolution in community. To learn more about this special mission, see the "Building Evolutionary Community" entry in the Recommended Resources section in Part IV.

Below, I present one proven method for getting started in forming an evolutionary community: Town Meetings in the Round.

Town Meetings in the Round

A key thesis of this book has been that a historic opportunity has been given to us: to create a new social model to guide us forward in making the Planetary Shift. The challenges we face are unprecedented; therefore, so must be the structure and processes. A crucial part of this work is the task of evolving our democratic processes so that they become what I call *synergistic democracy*. As with so many other activities in the Shift, the key to creating emergent governance structures lies in the word "synergy."

Town Meetings in the Round demonstrate social synergy in an important new way. Such town meetings are exciting events. They build community, create friendships, solve problems, and awaken previously unknown potentials in a local setting.

How to Get Started with a Town Meeting:
Town Meetings in the Round can take place in a school, a church, or even in a grassy field. The first step is to

establish a coordinating team. For example, a core group of those who are already involved in creating Evolutionary Shift Circles in a locality or region can join together to call a Town Meeting in their community, and then form a steering committee. If this sounds a bit daunting, just remember what the Occupy movement accomplished in a few weeks. Like them, we too can self-assemble far more easily than ever before; we too have the technology and the sense of urgency that motivates us to seek cooperative solutions. In fact, let's go a step further and help the Occupy movement grow into an "Evolve" movement—a new model for social synergy in any community!

Activities of a Town Meeting:

As they enter the meeting, the attendees should gather in a large wheel-like formation. A general facilitator opens by reminding everyone of the meeting's purpose. In the past we have actually launched Town Meetings by creating a "theater for the future" to dramatize our community-building intention, with offerings of music, poetry, and theater provided by local artists. Show your Town Meeting that all the world is a stage and everyone *really* is a player!

People can then be invited to self-organize based on vocational interests in the various sectors of the Wheel of Cocreation. Bear in mind that placing oneself in a sector provides members of your community with a great opportunity for "vocational dating," that is, finding new cocreative partners and teammates within the Wheel, and beginning to match their own needs with others' resources.

Your sectors can be named differently than they are named in the Wheel, but make sure you have selected the vital functions of your community. Think of the sectors as "organs" for vital functional fields in the emerging local social body, and follow your common sense to create sectors such as health, education, environment, governance, science, and technology.

When meetings in sectors conclude, sector leaders report to the whole assembly. Remember that in such meetings we are exploring the "planetary DNA" as we create a more synergistic democracy designed for cooperation and cocreation. In the Town Meetings in the Round we are contributing to social evolution, with *ourselves* as agents for the Planetary Shift. To find out more about the Town Meeting process, please go to Birth2012.com and also see the "Cocreative Society" entry in the Recommended Resources section in Part IV.

The First Syncons: A Forecast of What We Can Do Together Now

The original process that led to the concept of Town Meetings in the Round began with the work of my Washington, DC, based Committee for the Future, back in the 1970s. We created twenty-five such events for all sorts of communities, including gang leaders in Los Angeles; space scientists in Huntsville, Alabama; diplomats in Washington, DC, and seaside with people from Jamaica at the invitation of the Jamaican Prime Minister. At that time, we called these face-to-face meetings "SYNCONs," standing for SYNergistic CONvergence; as indicated earlier, we now use the term "Syncons."

Why did we organize so many Syncons? Remember, nature is a hierarchy of synergistic convergence. We have learned from Prigogine that nonlinear connectivity of what is novel jumps a system to a higher order. The first Syncons were prototypes of new social structures that actually fostered diverse groups coming together to form a whole system greater than the sum of its parts. Our early Syncons were harbingers of what today might become a more synergistic democratic process at all levels, including global.

In this book, and in the Birth 2012 Campaign, I offer a vision of the early phases of how to achieve global social synergy, which is now urgently needed as a way to connect what is working as we enter the age of conscious evolution. Syncons model this work in microcosm. So, allow me to share just a bit of history to catch a glimpse of the excitement and power of the original Syncon process. As we pursue the Birth 2012 Campaign we can refer to this earlier experience; we can improve upon and evolve the Syncon concept to meet today's needs.

The first Syncon was held at Southern Illinois University in 1972. My friend Buckminster Fuller was a scholar-in-residence at that time, and the son of my partner John Whiteside was a student there. As you'll remember, this was a period of massive social protests on college campuses. Students were locking up deans and tearing down universities. Everyone seemed to dislike everyone else. For example, the environmentalists hated technologists, blacks hated whites, scientists distrusted psychics. The "planetary baby," still in the womb of self-centered consciousness, had an allergy against itself. One part of the social body got hives at the very thought of another!

Without being directed, the students who helped produce our inaugural Syncon constructed a three-dimensional Wheel of Cocreation: a large circular environment with removable walls between sectors. The walls were decorated by art students to represent the different sectors. It looked like a UFO had landed at Southern Illinois University! At the Hub of the Wheel the students built a spiral staircase, allowing people to climb up and look down at the social Wheel as a whole system—and catch a glimpse of the "planetary DNA" at work.

This historic Syncon at Southern Illinois University was an amazing event. Warren Avis, founder of Avis Rent-a-Car, attended. He said it was like the party where you could meet everyone you wanted to in your community, but whom you ordinarily wouldn't dare to approach! At first, the Black Power leaders in long African robes who were present mingled uneasily with the chief economist of the U.S. Chamber of Commerce. Students confronted professors. Environmentalists scorned business leaders. The poor rejected the rich. But John Whiteside divined a process that overcame this division. His goal and mine was to create more energy through synergy than through opposition. This approach was not especially idealistic, but instead amounted to a new pragmatism. We were learning that each part gains something more by joining rather than by opposing—in other words, that synergy creates more energy since a synergized whole is greater than the sum of its parts.

Each sector was guided by a knowledgeable facilitator who asked the participants to state their goals, needs, and resources. Then various sectors were asked to enter into dialogue; they were directed to seek common goals and match needs with resources. Gradually, through a process of scheduled mergers, corollary but apparently conflicting functional groups met—such as environmentalists with technologists or business people with welfare mothers—all stating what they wanted to create, and finding others who needed what they had to give to achieve their own vision. At the end, all sectors met in an Assembly of the Whole where the entire Syncon continued the process of matching needs with resources across sector lines to achieve common goals.

At one point in this event we invited leaders at the growing edge of scientific and psychological potential to meet in task forces in separate disciplines, and then to connect with each other to synthesize and offer an overview of unacknowledged breakthrough capacities. They later reported to the whole what it would be like if such emerging capacities became operational to meet social needs. Such specialty groups were called "growing-edge" task forces.

Imagine that innovations in biology, information science, physical and space sciences, and the psychologies of transformation were to merge and then be included in the effort both to realize untapped potentials as well as solve societal problems such as poverty, disease, and depression. What would happen? The answer became clear even in this first Syncon: We actually can solve almost any social crisis and realize radical new capacities in the process.

As we take the next turn on the Spiral, we can extend our productivity, become far more intelligent, realize our psychological creativity, prolong our life span, free ourselves from repetitive work, and explore the mysteries of inner and outer space. We can envision that Maslow's hierarchy of needs—deficiency needs, growth needs, and needs for transcendence—could be met simultaneously, empowering everyone to a new level of creativity. The possible human and the possible society will be revealed, to use Jean Houston's terms. In our near future, mythical visions will merge into evolutionary potentiality!

At the first Syncon, a new evolutionary pragmatism and powerful visions of such a positive future inspired everyone with new hopes. Artists were also invited to this Syncon (and to every Syncon we held subsequently). They would symbolically encircle both the Wheel and the growing-edge task forces. Their purpose was to help the social body see and experience itself as a whole. These artists, playwrights, poets, and musicians later told us how grateful they were to be included in a social environment where people were actually struggling to evolve, instead of only having their artistic creations being seen in galleries, museums, or theaters. This experience could be likened to the medieval times when artists, inspired by one great story, built the magnificent cathedrals of Europe. Now, these artists at Syncon said, we have a new story; it is the Universe Story, the story of our own evolution toward greater consciousness, freedom, and order.

We soon came to see that the Syncon model reveals our potential in embryo, in a kind of "social cosmogenesis." Not only does the universe show up as each of us in person, it also manifests collectively as we cluster together to form new whole systems of universal potentiality. Today, new art forms are being engendered by our new story—in films and in music, art, dance, and poetry. Once these art forms begin to burst out upon the public mind, I believe the great convergence will accelerate.

The highlight of every Syncon was our All Walls Down ceremony. At the first Syncon, the actress Nichelle Nichols, who had played Lieutenant Uhura in Star Trek, stood in the Hub of the Wheel and sang, "Joshua Fought the Battle of Jericho and the Walls Came a-Tumbling Down." People started to actually spiral around her in a dance.

As we learned even in the first Syncon and thereafter, it didn't matter at all what assumptions and prejudices people had held about each other when a Syncon started. As the weekend came to a close, a feeling of awe always took over. Linkages among formerly conflicting groups spread like ripples in a pond while the reports from the growing-edge sciences and psychologies stimulated a self-revelation of the social body to itself. We caught a glimpse of what we can be, which is so much greater than what we are actually doing or even imagining.

By the end, an awareness of our common potentials infused participants. Stereotypes disappeared. We experienced radical amazement. Like macro-molecules becoming a cell, or cells becoming multi-cells, we were fusing into a new whole where all parts got to be more of who they wanted to become. We were synergizing.

Each Syncon we convened was almost a social love affair. The astronaut Edgar Mitchell attended a Syncon and during the All Walls Down ceremony said that if we had had a spiritual Geiger counter it would have gone off the charts. This perception should come as no surprise if you remember that the Latin root of the word "religion" is *re-ligare*, to bind back and make whole. Synergistic convergence is essentially a spiritual/social joining that *naturally* fosters wholeness, thus satisfying a longing that persists in all of us no matter our apparent differences. "Union differentiates," as Teilhard de Chardin once said. Uniqueness is increased through synergy.

Among other dignitaries I invited to the first Syncon in Carbondale, Illinois was a diplomat named Laizar Moisov. An Ambassador from Yugoslavia, he was then head of the United Nations Security Council in New York City. During that weekend, he worked with the group in the governance sector of the Wheel.

We wisely decided that there was to be no star treatment for celebrities or people of status. They all simply operated in a functional section of the Wheel according to their vocation. Every now and then they were invited to speak to the whole group, but always from their own sectors. In this way, the old social architecture of speakers upfront lecturing to rows of passive listeners was changed to enhance cooperation. The large structured Wheel itself was a statement of a new social orientation toward synergy.

Ambassador Moisov said afterwards that the United Nations should use the Syncon model. The United Nations as it was currently structured, he told us, could not work because it was comprised of nation-states that were acting not on behalf of the world's people but to protect their country's national sovereignty. He pointed out that the General Assembly and the Security Council were also organized into oppositional forces not unlike our democracy in the United States. He invited John and I to what was then Yugoslavia to facilitate a Syncon, but Yugoslav President Tito would not allow it.

Jumping ahead to the mid-1980s, I want to note that lessons like those we learned in Illinois and at other Syncons were reinforced when I travelled to the former Soviet Union as a citizen diplomat. I helped organize the first Soviet-American Citizens' Summit in Moscow, which was hosted by the Center for Soviet-American Dialogue and led by Rama Vernon. This event used the Syncon model. Americans and Soviets were invited into sectors of the Wheel to develop joint projects. The bureaucracies behind both the American State Department and the Soviet Peace Committee said it would never work! Actually, it worked so well that people experienced a mutual love that allowed them to begin to cocreate with no attention at all paid to ideologies.

The same situation also occurred when we brought gang leaders of Los Angeles into the Wheel along with police officers, welfare mothers, and science fiction writers like Gene Roddenberry of Star Trek and Ray Bradbury. At one point, ABC newsmen came into the Syncon with their cameras, and attempted to take the young gang members aside to be videotaped. But one of the young men said to ABC News: "STOP! We won't let you do this to us again. We won't let you film us as the ones who are wrong and violent." Our own cameras filmed him resisting the ABC News people. When they left, we filmed him with our small hand-held cameras. He turned to us and said, "I think it's going to be okay . . . I think we'll be heard."

Today we can turn to advanced twenty-first-century digital tools to create Syncons, both as local events or on the Internet.

My partner in this great work of creating Syncons was Lt. Col. John Whiteside, who had been Chief Officer for Information for the Air Force before he joined me to cofound the Committee for the Future in 1970. He had pioneered in conceiving and producing the live TV coverage of the Apollo Program—a novel idea at that time—and knew how to produce large events. During the first Syncon at Southern Illinois University he placed small hand-held television cameras at the Hub of the Wheel. I had sold my home in Lakeville, Connecticut, and bought these cameras with the proceeds from the sale. I haven't owned a real home since; instead, I have become and remain a Wheel builder!

John also invented a "Synconsole," a "social-mission control system" based on NASA's Houston Mission Control. The Synconsole had a screen for every sector of the wheel. It was an internal nervous system for the social body, so people could sense themselves as part of the whole, even though each was focusing on a specific part. Whenever someone agreed on something new, our cameras rushed in to document the breakthrough.

John directed the story of our convergence from the Hub of the Wheel. Every evening he and the SIU students edited a TV show called *The New World's Evening News*, which highlighted convergences, sudden agreements, and creative linkage, instead of the usual emphasis on breakdowns and violence. People saw themselves as the news, and wanted to watch themselves *as* the news over and over again.

After engaging in dialogue with my husband and me, our idea that "our story is the birth of a universal humanity" awakened in John his own greater life purpose. We gave him Earl's book, *The Search Is On*, which as you'll recall I edited from our breakfast dialogues. He soon quit the Air Force and joined Earl and me to actually help develop a new way to realize long-range evolutionary goals. Together, we originated the Syncon method as a significant step in social synergy.

In 1982, John died of cancer. I was with him just when he died, and witnessing his passing was as great a miracle as a birth.

In my grief, I felt his presence . . .

"Where did you go, John?" I whispered to him.

"I'm gone to create the Great Syncon in the sky. I'll be ready when you need me!"

John, I believe the time is now.

A Vision of the Future Equal to Our Potential

Here we are! At the new beginning, celebrating Birth 2012 and what comes beyond it: humanity's Great Shift to the age of conscious evolution. We are countless millions of people coming together to participate in the planetary birthing process. We should have a Planetary Birth Day every year to mark the progress of humanity toward its potential, just as we celebrate Earth Day every year.

Let us also envision that we will initiate an ongoing Virtual Global Syncon. It will be anchored locally in Town Meetings and facilitated by pioneers in every sector of the Wheel and in every region of the world. In turn, Town Meetings in the Round will be anchored in Shift Circles of all kinds.

As we meet, we will guide each other to state our goals, needs, and resources—either on the Internet or in face-to-face gatherings. We will ask questions of each other and draw upon the collective genius now encoded in the great search engines of the world.

The Wheel will be filled with projects now working in every field and function. They will self-organize according to specific functions in every "organ" of our social body. For example, in the sector of education there will be clusters on the education of youth, of the aged, of the disabled, of the gifted. Each vocational cluster will be in conversation with others who share that vocation— and will conclude by convening to consider the capacities of the emerging whole within their sector.

There will also be a continuing communication of the "new news" of what is working in each sector. Around the Wheel, networks of networks will connect via the Internet.

People and processes in the Hub of the Wheel will serve to cultivate care and respect for one another, to support each other in their shifting from ego to essence, to discover their deeper vocations, to find their partners, to connect functionally, and to match needs with resources globally. They too will communicate the new news continually.

The great vision of the Planetary Peace Room will come alive. A Peace Room can exist in every locale that is represented on the Internet. People can join together in living rooms and schools everywhere to scan for, map, connect, and communicate what is working in their respective communities. They will provide energetic support for this work by entering into heart coherence in their Evolutionary Shift Circles.

The great mythmakers and storytellers of Hollywood and Bollywood will celebrate our new myth and tell the stories of what is working, what is being born. A new form of "elders from the future" will emerge as local "Welcoming Committees," welcoming each community forward toward its emergence.

Ultimately, it is hardly imaginable how vast and potent we can be. The terrible problems of hunger, disease, war, resource depletion—so painful during our transition to becoming a universal cocreative humanity—will not so much be "solved" as evolved naturally through the synergy of our creativity. We will find our way through together.

Let us therefore call upon the innate genius and the heart's desire of humanity to consciously evolve. The Shift Network is helping point the way. Birth 2012 is an invitation to participate in a first baby step of a planetary species seeking to live in love as we cocreate the Planetary Shift.

In this book we have traced an arc of evolution from the great cosmic story to our own personal, small-group, and large-scale social participation in the evolutionary journey, as agents of conscious evolution.

We *are* connecting heart with heart and center with center, waking up within a field of love in our global heart. The living noosphere is getting its collective eyes! Let us envision that by December 22, 2012, we will have established a great ongoing synergistic experiment. As the "small fluctuations in the sea of social chaos," we will have finally gathered together to jump our world to a whole-system shift.

Through the Birth 2012 Campaign we are helping to make visible the invisible, celebrating what is being born through all of us. We see the outlines of ourselves growing up as a Universal Humanity when our spiritual, social, scientific, and technological capacities are integrated.

As we lean into the future, casting our weight upon the waves of change, we seek humbly to be guided by the universal process that is forever unfolding.

The *new* good news is, we are now *intentionally* co-creating humanity's Great Shift to the age of conscious evolution.

As an early pioneer in conscious evolution I am filled with gratitude and joy to participate with you in this marvelous adventure into the unknown future, animated by the flame of expectation in our hearts.

 *Afterword*

Our Journey into the Birth and Beyond

By Stephen Dinan, CEO and founder,
The Shift Network

To envision a collective Birth movement that will ultimately engage more than 100 million people worldwide requires courage and a lot of trust. I sometimes shake my head in disbelief at the very idea of The Shift Network bringing this movement together and creating ways for millions to participate. However, the resounding "yes!" we have received at each stage of our work convinces me that we are on the right track.

We have pursued this mission because I trust Barbara Marx Hubbard's long-held vision and her clear inner guidance, as well as the original vision for The Shift Network that I was given during a meditation retreat in 2000, and also other "downloads" since. I trust that the tens of thousands who have listened to our calls—or the thousands who have devoted time, resources, and energy to becoming Agents of Conscious Evolution through our courses—are responding to an innate power in the idea of the Birth movement. I also trust that when many traditions and lineages have prophetically declared 2012 as a time of unprecedented change, then something quite real must be underway.

Humility comes from recognizing that we are not causing the Birth so much as providing a positive pathway for those who want to participate in what is already evolving. We can help to "gentle the transition," as Barbara writes, thereby making it "across the gap" as peacefully and gracefully as possible. We can connect what is working and amplify the good that is happening in the world. We can even make the transition more joyful. Ultimately, though, the drive towards a planetary birth comes from forces larger than we can understand with our intellect.

Each one of us seems so small and the currents of history so powerful that it can feel daunting to try to make a positive impact. However, the truth is that every major evolution in history has been ignited from a small group of people who then expanded their influence in ever-widening circles. And with the advent of the Internet and mass media, our capacity for collective transformation has increased exponentially. As pointed out in this book, within just a few weeks in the fall of 2011, Occupy Wall Street mushroomed into a global movement, capturing the public imagination worldwide.

What if we can do the same, beginning in 2012 and going beyond, not just as a protest against the old but as a celebratory birth of the new? And what if we can make it wildly creative, outrageously fun, and attractive to more and more people?

The truth is that we *can* create a large-scale birthing journey, each stage taking us to another level of maturation, peaking with the Planetary Birth Day event and continuing to evolve into the future.

This is what we are designing and inviting you to cocreate with us. In the following pages, I will take you through our current vision for the Birth 2012 Campaign and beyond. The final story, however, will be written through the creativity and participation of millions, including you. The seeds we plant, the events we ignite, and the infrastructure we provide is only a platform upon which people like you will create something far more profound and important. In these pages, I will only focus on the initiatives that we at The Shift Network are directly activating, but be assured that the Birth will be composed of thousands of interrelated projects, all of which are essential. Some of these initiatives are listed in Part IV of the book, Resources for the Birth.

With that said, let us begin.

Conception Day: March 22, 2012

All birth begins with conception, the fertilization of new life, when the unique DNA of two join together as one. A sperm completes its heroic journey to unite with an egg and their evolutionary impulse finds fruition in a new being. That is why we begin our Birth 2012 journey with a global Conception Day on March 22, 2012, exactly nine months before the Birth Day. What a joyous moment—the conception of new life—but in this case, the new life of all of humanity!

Most of you who are reading this will be seeing this day in the rearview mirror of history. So, let me explain what we had envisioned happening on Conception Day and speak about it in the past tense: We saw it as a large-scale fertilization of the Birth movement made up of people from around the world drawing inspiration from Barbara Marx Hubbard and the Welcoming Committee—and then used it to draw together like-minded local cocreators with whom they joined in manifesting their unique gifts over the ensuing nine months.

To use one of Barbara Marx Hubbard's favorite phrases, we also saw Conception Day as a day for what Barbara calls suprasex, the joining of our collective genius to cocreate rather than combining our genes to procreate. Of course, suprasex is not limited to this single day. We do it every time we open ourselves to true collaboration, sincere sharing, or real partnership. Conception Day was a way to celebrate suprasex on a large scale (and enjoy the lightness and fun of the Birth).

Suprasexual conception of a planetary birth— how irresistible is that?

The Nine-Month Gestation

Conception is, of course, always followed by gestation—the growth of the fetus in the womb. In utero, the baby grows cell by cell, organ by organ. In the same sense, we expect that during every day of the nine-month gestation, the Birth movement will grow and its participants—like the cells or organs of a new humanity—will offer more of their gifts to create it, thus building the collective "baby" little by little.

To accelerate the weaving together of the global movement, we are providing a Daily Heart Shift that allows transformational teachers to share their wisdom on how we can come together in a spirit of oneness. This presentation is followed by Heart Lock-In practice, the HeartMath technique discussed in Chapter 4 that involves creating heart coherence at a deeper level, then sending that energy to others. We end each session with some minutes of shared intention for healing specific areas of the world. This last act of subtle activism—sending heartfelt care to places around the world—creates a side benefit of joining us together in a spirit of shared compassion.

This Daily Heart Shift can give us an anchor point in each day that will help us shift from our separate concerns to remembering ourselves as one shared planetary consciousness that is waking up together. In addition to this Daily Heart Shift, we offer what we call Shift Packs—mobile media releases of short videos, audios, and articles designed to help us each deepen our shift to a new way of being and to manifest those changes in the world. The idea is that in the midst of our busy lives, we can take a few minutes to shift to a deeper state of being. As we do this again and again, we learn to stabilize ourselves within a new way of being.

Forming Evolutionary Shift Circles

On our social network, ShiftMovement.com, online groups are now forming into online clusters of interest and passion, helping to interconnect those with shared vocations or visions. In addition, as Barbara indicated earlier, people around the world are creating in-person local Evolutionary Shift Circles that meet weekly to focus on different aspects of the personal and collective changes that are required for the Planetary Shift, and some of these are specialized as peace circles or men's and women's groups. Shift Circles are creating a shared field of resonance and deep purpose for Birth 2012.

With each new day, then, the heart and minds of those drawn to participate in the collective Birth are becoming more intimately woven together, allowing us to see, feel, and operate from the oneness at the core of what Barbara calls the Hub. We are thus beginning to experience the Birth in miniature, through circles of loving resonance and cocreation. As we experience the shifts ourselves, we increase our capacity to guide and inspire others. Through working with a few friends in small circles, you can mirror what needs to happen on a larger scale: all of us joining together as a more global whole. In this way, you can become extremely valuable to the Planetary Birth experience on December 22.

As more of us join into resonant circles, we will be empowered to more fully give our greatest gifts to the Shift. Each of us has what can be thought of as "soul DNA"—we come in with higher intentions for our incarnation that predisposes us for specific skills and talents. We might be coded to paint, to start a business, to teach, or to write. We may take a lifetime to muster the courage to follow these impulses from our souls and manifest our most heartfelt dreams, but when we do, we are energized at the deepest level of our being and can create real impact.

The Spring of Sustainability

As part of focusing our attention on the collective birthing process, The Shift Network envisions several "seasons" of special activities that model the shift to a new culture. First, we see the global Shift movement taking on concrete, positive change initiatives through activating the Spring of Sustainability, a season whose goal is to bring us back into harmony with the earth. This sequence of events begins with Conception Day and continues to June 22, the first day of the Summer of Peace. During this period, we will generate inspiring media, telesummits, and public calls for collective action, all designed to move us joyfully toward greater sustainability as a movement. We anticipate local potlucks, tree plantings, and large-scale commitments to carbon offsets. We envision new organic gardens, healthier school lunches, and policy changes at the national level—and much more.

The Summer of Peace

We at The Shift Network see the momentum building in an accelerated way during the Summer of Peace, beginning precisely six months before the Birth on June 22, 2012. We are envisioning those six months as the largest season of commitment on behalf of peace that has ever occurred on planet Earth. During this period, we see

millions making a profound personal pledge to nonviolence, spreading the science and practice of peace, and
engaging in acts of reconciliation with our brothers and
sisters on a level never seen before. In three months, we
can make a powerful leap forward in advancing practices
that foster peace in schools, communities, and homes, as
well as advocating for major policy changes in governments that have the potential of establishing peace as the
new norm.

We see the establishment of dozens of new Cities of
Peace worldwide that share best practices and curricula
for making their cities oases of peace. Furthermore, we
envision areas of active conflict in the world participating
through ceasefires and truces. At a smaller scale, individuals can participate by creating neighborhood circles and
events, spreading peace media virally, and advocating for
shifts in schools, businesses, and cities.

The deeper logic of the Summer of Peace and its relationship to the global Birth is this: In order to prepare
for the Birth, it is essential that we first release the past
and bear witness to all the oppression, disharmony, and
destruction that has gone before us. During the Summer
of Peace, the goal is for us to own, forgive, heal, and
move on, in a giant season of cleansing our history. As
the global collaborations for peace grow, they will culminate in a particularly powerful International Day of
Peace on September 22, just three months from the Planetary Birth. If all goes well, major global concerts will be
performed. As I write this, for example, the creators of
Live Aid are working to activate a global Superconcert
in ten cities that reaches hundreds of millions from September 21–23.

On the International Day of Peace, the "Push-
4Peace" campaign will also launch, headed up by
Welcoming Committee member Dot Maver. All of the
power generated from the Summer of Peace can, we
believe, be turned into ninety days of real changes in

the policies and practices of governments, schools, and businesses worldwide. By this point, the global fetus will be six months old, taking on the shape and features of a fully developed child. Just as the senses of the child develop, we'll have radio and TV platforms chronicling evolutionary processes and tools, allowing participants to amplify their own contributions.

The Autumn of Abundance

Finally, I see the momentum growing still further through an Autumn of Abundance during the last three months, with an outpouring of generosity worldwide. At the foundation of the work of building a new global society is the rebalancing of our economic systems by spreading greater prosperity and creating an economic system that rewards those who are doing good for the world.

For example, we envision the large-scale activation of microlending funds, entrepreneurial trainings, and the stirring of a larger gift economy. Tom Coleman of the Bottom Billion Fund estimates that with just 100 billion dollars, we could create a nonprofit micro-enterprise fund that serves the financing needs of the *entire* "bottom billion" of the world. Imagine the billionaire pledge begun by Warren Buffet and Bill Gates spreading to well-to-do millionaires worldwide—leading many to come together in a season of profound commitment to helping the world's poor begin to thrive.

On the programming front, we'll launch a free and very large Enlightened Business Summit, making the best wisdom for creating enlightened companies available to everyone throughout the world.

For the Autumn of Abundance we see a profound focus on sharing with others, opening the channels of giving that have often been closed. What if, no matter our level of wealth, we each pledged to sponsor one child's education or even a school in the developing world? What if we dare each other to take wild new leaps of generosity in our own communities?

This season will also provide an opportune time to address systemic changes that get corporations out of politics and build greater trust through increased transparency. Finally, in the latter part of this season, we expect to see *The Shift Movie* released to the public with its poetic, energizing tribute to the growing global movement, showcasing many of the key leaders, ideas, and initiatives.

Navigating the Turbulence

Throughout this nine months of gestation, I suspect that we will continue to see social unrest the likes of which will make the year 2011 seem calm. The grassroots movements for change will likely surge in even stronger ways as the cracks widen in the old systems, causing them to break down.

While this is happening, those of us who follow Barbara's vision will experience this as a birthing time and we will have solace. For us, the societal earthquakes can be seen as part of a higher purpose to create space for the "pioneering souls" and their innovations to emerge. A birth is usually a messy business, and shaking off centuries of old habits will be a challenging process. Our nine-month collective birthing will, I suspect, take place concurrently with economic malaise, environmental calamity, social unrest, and more. There will be resistance to the evolutionary changes as well as to those who try to pull things back to the stability of the old order.

As we navigate through this time of deep challenge, it will be key for us to find our calm center, the part of us that knows it is all in divine hands as the outdated structures crumble and fall away. Something magnificent will be taking shape. A golden future awaits us. As we anchor that knowledge in our own hearts, we can become pillars of strength for others and help them see instability through the eyes of opportunity for collective growth.

The Planetary Birth Day Celebration

And that brings us to the Planetary Birth Day itself, December 22, 2012, the first day of the next 5,125-year Mayan calendar, an auspicious moment to declare a symbolic birth. December 22 is also the day after Winter Solstice, when the light begins its return from the darkest night, a perfect setting for collective rebirth—the light of Divinity shining more strongly again through each and every soul. It will also be the day after a wide range of other collaborating groups have staged massive concerts, performed a global "song" in unison, held worldwide meditations, and more, in an effort to make December 21 visible and powerful.

However, our particular focus is on the 22nd —Day One of the next era. Just as with typical New Year's celebrations, the eve is the time to party out the old, and the next day is the time to set intentions for the coming year. In a parallel fashion, we will use December 22 as the time to set our collective intentions for a new era of peace, sustainability, health, and the emergence of a Universal Humanity. The Birth Day will represent a global coming together of humanity in a spirit of oneness through broadcasts, concerts, unifying spiritual practices, conscious service, great "gifting" of each other, and commitments to international citizenship.

We envision a global broadcast to open the Birth Day: Barbara giving a State of the Planet address, luminaries sharing their latest breakthroughs, and an unforgettable display of our one-hundred-year vision for the future. Beyond the broadcast, we foresee holding special periods of globally linked spiritual practices—prayer, meditation, song, sound, and sacred dance, from Sufi dervish twirling to Tibetan chanting. The power of these circles of simultaneous spiritual practice around the world will ensure that these moments of shared resonance reverberate far and wide.

As the day progresses, we see the lighting of torches in every time zone, forming a global Birth Day cake. And what would a birthday celebration be without gifts? Since we are *all* being born, we will all gift each other in spontaneous and abundant ways. From One World Potlucks to all-night dance parties, we see the evening as a time for global community and celebration, recognizing ourselves as one human family celebrating a global Holy Day together in the midst of the season of so many other holidays.

We also envision mass signings of a commitment to global interdependence, signifying that we are moving beyond competitive individualism to healthy cooperation on which human civilization can now be built. We envision heads of states and of the United Nations making this commitment, so that the new era can be one in which we are making interdependence the fundamental truth, balancing individual and collective good. Finally, participants will all receive a Birth Certificate, certifying them as newly born members of the global family.

This vision is far from complete. We know that others will complement our work by developing their own ideas. For example, why not create the largest Samba line in history, simultaneous hula dancing, or comedy marathons? We especially want to encourage artists and entertainers to pioneer new ways to mark this moment and create memorable ways for people to participate. The key will be to blend collective simultaneous actions that promote a sense of global unity, with individual creativity that supports the flowering of the human spirit in novel forms. This is the social artistry of the next era.

Again, our goal is for 100 million people to participate in some aspect of the Planetary Birth Day. Why? That number represents a bit more than one percent of our global population, and some intriguing science suggests that one percent of any solution or structure can be enough to shift the pattern of the whole. This small percentage is an achievable goal and just may be enough to create a powerful collective effect.

If more than one percent of the world's population joins in the spirit of global oneness on this day, will we see something like the phase shift that happens in supersaturated solutions? Will we glimpse a new pattern and thus be inspired to make the Shift real in the coming decades?

With the successful creation of this vision, we believe that December 22, 2012, will always be remembered as the beginning, as DAY ONE, the moment when the people of planet Earth decided to jointly reach for our higher purpose and declare the beginning of a new era.

However, as with the birth of a baby, the Birth Day is only the beginning of a long phase of unfolding. We must learn to eat, speak, crawl, run, and much more, if we are to become a successful human being—or a newly born planet. So must the changes activated during the nine-month collective birthing be allowed a period of maturation over years and decades in order to develop to fruition. That's why we expect that December 22 will be celebrated every year thereafter as we renew the commitments made on the day of Birth.

From 2012 to 2020 and Beyond

The eight years after the Birth, leading up to 2020, will be critical for implementing the shifts necessary for us to gently grow into the next era and overcome the crises we face without having to endure a hard landing. This will be a time in which the systems that were once breaking down begin to finally shift to a more holistic, integrated, and balanced pattern, with renewed goals for our education system, improved guidelines for conscious enterprise, innovative methods for creating participatory democracy, and more advanced opportunities for creating religious unity. I see us building the foundations of health, peace, sustainability, and prosperity into the core systems of our world. I see the cocreative Shift Circles of 2012 evolving into fully formed evolutionary communities and residential developments. I see centers springing up in locations around the world where each person can learn to transform themselves and our world.

Beyond 2012, I believe the mainstream media will also carry more of the good news of a new humanity. And our hearts will know that we have each done our very best to foster this breakthrough in human culture and consciousness. The master (and mother) memes will be set in motion, sculpting a worldview aligned with the Universal Human. Resilient, restorative communities will become increasingly common. And we will breathe a collective sigh of relief that we have, indeed, made the Shift in time to protect our beautiful world for future generations.

Part 3

WELCOMING
THE BIRTH

The Welcoming Committee Essays

Introducing the Welcoming Committee

The inspiration for the formation of the first Welcoming Committee comes deep from the heart of evolution.

The purpose of these twelve evolutionary pioneers is to welcome us through this critical and dangerous birthing process by the example and demonstrations of their lifework. From an evolutionary point of view, they may be signals for the noosphere that we are ready to be born—or rather that we are being born!

The kinds of signals that we now receive in our collective consciousness can be a decisive factor as to whether we have a gentle birth or experience a more violent transition. In a way, we are parenting ourselves through this process, both as members of the newly born culture and as guides for it. If in addition we can look to a group of twelve highly accomplished, loving, and wise guides who have volunteered for that role, it can make all the difference to our future. The Welcoming Committee plays just that new role, offering key elements of the pattern of the whole-system shift.

As you read the Welcoming Committee essays that follow you will see that each expresses an aspect of the new life and new consciousness now arising on Earth.

They welcome each of us to awaken to our own part in the Great Shift, to do what we are born to do, and to give our Gift to the Shift now.

As a group, our Welcoming Committee is seeking to reach up to a billion people by December 22, 2012, on behalf of the Birth Campaign. This alone may mean enough of us will be here to gentle the Birth to the next stage of our evolution. The Committee's very presence, its collective outreach, and the members' widespread popularity give all of us hope.

Each member of the Welcoming Committee is like a planetary midwife to the cosmic child that we potentially are: the new planetary culture that none of us has fully seen before. We hope they will inspire many communities throughout the world to form their own welcoming committees composed of key visionaries and pioneers in their locality or region. We envision welcoming committees connecting with other welcoming committees and filling the earth with vibrant seeds of new conscious life.

Finally, each essay in this section offers a vision for the organic growth potential of the new human and new humanity. You will find inspiration as to how to take our next steps toward peace and into a new cultural story, as well as cultivate a better relationship with indigenous peoples. You will discover suggestions for how our economy might turn the tide from ever-greater financial destabilization toward a global Marshall Plan. You will read about how to tap into our unlimited creativity, and how our spirituality is shifting us from the egocentric to the world-centric stage as we become architects of global change. The dangerous current "global bifurcation" will also be made clear, as well as how to rise above it. You will also explore those vital personal questions from Jack Canfield that we hope each of you will take the time to consider, the answers to which will provide you with your own guidelines for the birthing process.

—**Barbara Marx Hubbard**

Living on the Eve of the New Story

By Jean Houston

So, HERE WE ARE IN THE YEAR OF 2012, THE MYTHIC YEAR of *what?* Radical transition? Kingdom of Heaven? Ninth Circle of Hell? Opening Times coming close on the heels of Closing Times? Or could we be awakening from the chrysalis and emerging into new ways of being? What did those old Mayans really know, anyway?

Although there have been many births and deaths and rebirths of civilizations over the last five thousand years, the birth process we are witnessing in our time is far more radical than any previous births of new cultures out of old ones. We are endlessly confronted by the many seemingly impossible challenges of our time, the greatest being the threat of ecological breakdown; yet, we are constantly witnessing inspiring breakthroughs as people everywhere rise up to challenge the old patterns of the past. It's almost as if we are jumping off into a new dispensation. Clearly, whatever else this may be, we are in what I like to call "Jump Time."

Jump Time signifies the momentum behind the current drama of the world, the breakdown and breakthrough of every old way of being, knowing, relating, governing, and believing. It shakes the foundations of all and everything. And it allows for another order of reality to come into time. Jump Time is whole-system transition, a condition of interactive change that affects every aspect of life as we know it.

And yet, the vision of change that I hold is generally optimistic. It focuses on the emergence of patterns of possibility never before available to Earth's people as a whole. For example, we are embedded in a larger ecology of being, its motive force arising simultaneously from the planet, which is our birthplace, and from the stars, which are our destination. We are being pulsed by the Earth and the universe toward a new stage of growth. As Barbara Marx Hubbard so brilliantly shows us, we are waking up to the realization that we can become partners in creation—stewards of Earth's well-being and conscious participants in the cosmic epic of evolution. Indeed, the cosmos provides us with an evolutionary impulse that drives our growth and at the same time suggests how we might learn to ride and direct its energy.

Part of this pulse toward partnership demands that in the near future, in order to save the earth and preserve and stabilize its fragile ecosystem, we may have to engage in vast macro-engineering projects supplemented by the nano-engineering of the atmosphere and the lithosphere. We may someday even have to transfer off-planet industrial and power-generating concerns. Using archives of genetic materials, we may eventually learn how to reverse the decline in species by reconstructing the lost genotypes of many creatures that inhabited the earth. In other words, before we try to terraform Mars to make it habitable, we will have to terraform the Earth—to make it more Earth-like! How's that for starters?

Regenerating the Earth will require not only futuristic technologies, but another order of human abilities, one that necessitates not only a more comprehensive understanding of our responsibilities but also the ability to tap into the creative workshops of the mind to solve problems and to bring forth art, poetry, invention—to direct our moods, our emotions, and our relationships in ways that align us with our finest selves.

In addition, we will need new social containers to house our evolving humanity—new ways of being in community given a global society. This implies, does it not, a fundamental change in the nature of civilization, compelling a passage beyond the mindset and institutions of millennia? Critical to this reformation is a true partnership society, in which women join men in the full social agenda. Since women tend to emphasize process over product—*being* rather than *doing*, deepening rather than end-goaling—it is inevitable that as a result of this partnership, our current reliance on linear, sequential solutions will yield to a way of knowing that comes from seeing things in whole constellations rather than as discrete facts. The holistic consciousness engendered by such a comprehensive vision would be better adapted to orchestrating the multiple variables and the multicultural realities of the modern world.

So, what is needed here is our willingness to cocreate a new social paradigm in which humanity and Earth are each embraced in a shared destiny. As old forms break down, a more complex and inclusive global organism comes into being. We are the living cells within this new organism, rescaled to earth-wide proportions in our responsiveness—and our responsibilities. We engage in the use of sacred rituals and technologies of consciousness, accessing the interconnected world as if it were an evolving world self. We thereupon discover the World Child, bearing the World Mind—a kind of cosmic fetus in each of us that must be nurtured in its infancy as it is protected in its development.

Getting rescaled to our new proportions and their responsibilities will also require that we each possess a psyche and spirit deep enough to sustain all this change; happily, these depths are breaking through most apparently in the spiritual renaissance that is occurring everywhere in Jump Time. And, what with the inevitable cross-fertilization of the wisdom and practices of world spiritual traditions, more and more people are gaining access to the Source of our being and becoming.

As this new story begins to take hold, the mytho-poetic insights of many cultures rise and converge. Archetypal ideas and symbols spring into consciousness or are consciously sought in the popular culture. The thought and work of Barbara Marx Hubbard has provided a fertile field for these archetypal ideas and symbols and beings to grow, and indeed, to become our partners in the great work of new creation.

Jean Houston is an American scholar, lecturer, author, and philosopher who has helped pioneer and motivate the human potential movement. As a teacher and visionary thinker, Houston holds conferences and seminars with social leaders, educational institutions, and business organizations worldwide. She has worked in over forty cultures and one hundred countries, helping leaders maintain cultural uniqueness as their countries become part of the global community. Houston has written or co-written nearly thirty books, including Jump Time: Shaping Your Future in a World of Radical Change.

The Overhaul of Humanity

By Neale Donald Walsch

WE BEGIN WITH A HYPOTHESIS:

> *The world is not the way we wish it were.*
> *Life on our planet is not the way we want it to be.*

If that hypothesis is false, there's nothing further to discuss. We are getting exactly what we want. If, on the other hand, the supposition is accurate, we continue with a question:

> *How is it possible for seven billion human beings*
> *to all desire the same thing*
> *(peace, security, opportunity, prosperity,*
> *happiness, and love)*
> *and to be unable to collectively produce it…*
> *even after trying for thousands of years?*

If that question produces no answer, no response that definitively clarifies the matter, we move to an unavoidable conclusion:

> *There is something we do not*
> *fully understand about life,*
> *the understanding of which would change everything.*

That is, in fact, what is so. It explains why life on Earth is and has been what it is and has been. Yet today there is news. We understand now what we did not understand before. Or more correctly, what we knew intuitively and expressed instinctively before, at the level of each of our individual cells, we have now come to comprehend cognitively and to express intentionally at the Whole Being level. We understand that We Are All One. We understand that as billions of individual cells are a part of our body, so, too, are we cells in the Body of God.

This understanding is, *in fact*, changing everything. It is producing what I have called the Overhaul of Humanity.

The word "overhaul" carries an interesting meaning. An overhaul is not a disassembling or a dismembering or a dismantling; the dictionary defines the word as "a thorough examination of machinery or a system, with repairs or changes made if necessary."

Now this phenomenon is going to involve (indeed, has already involved) every aspect of our lives: our governance and politics, our economics and financial stability, our commerce and industry, our social conventions and constructions, our educational systems and approaches, our religions and beliefs, our customs and traditions—in fact, our entire Cultural Story. Yet it can be the greatest thing that has happened to our species since our appearance on this planet.

The years just ahead, and some of the trials and tribulations we've already seen, can bring our planet to a new and wonderful place when the process is complete. Yes, there have been and will be challenges and loss. And it is right and proper to honor the souls who have suffered and died so that our species may continue to evolve. Yet this is not the End Times. Just the opposite. As my dear friend (and one of our civilization's greatest futurists and visionaries) Barbara Marx Hubbard puts it, this is not the death of us, but the *birthing* of us; the emergence of humanity into the cosmic community of sentient beings. All that has gone before has been, to use her words, our gestation.

The question now is, what shall become of us? If we are truly just being birthed, into what will we grow?

Ah, yes . . . well, that will depend on us. I dislike being as flat out trite as this, but: the future is in our hands. It depends on what we all decide about tomorrow. I would like to offer some suggestions as we work together to create humanity's New Cultural Story.

But wait, let's step back just a bit. *Create Humanity's New Cultural Story?* Yes. Allow me to explain.

Moments after the events of 9/11, I tearfully asked God how such things could have occurred—and what would prevent the human race from repeating such behaviors.

I should explain that I have been asking God these kinds of questions for a long time. Since mid-1992, when, in a moment of deep personal frustration, I called out to God, wrote an angry letter on a yellow legal pad—and began receiving answers to every question I ever had.

A movie was made of this, and the story has been told many times in the media since a book emerged from my experience, called *Conversations with God.*

(Some people might have a little trouble with this whole idea, particularly if they think that God stopped talking to humanity two thousand years ago or that, if God *has* continued communicating, it's been only with holy men, medicine women, or someone who has been meditating for thirty years or has been very good for twenty or at least half-decent for ten (none of which categories include me).

What I have learned, however, is that God talks to everyone. The good and the bad. The saint and the scoundrel. And certainly all of us in between. We are simply calling it something else. "Women's intuition." "Serendipity." A "moment of inspiration." A "brilliant idea." A "stroke of genius." A "blinding insight." An "epiphany!" And on and on it goes, with us using endlessly imaginative labels to describe something very simple: a connection with our Higher Self, which in turn is tuned into the wisdom of the ages through its connection with the Divine.

In response to my question following 9/11, God was very clear in her wording. He said that we must rewrite humanity's Cultural Story.

This is the story that we tell ourselves about ourselves. It is our notion of what it means to be human. It is our idea, our foundational thesis, around who and what we are, why we are here, and how we might best achieve the goals of our civilization. All of that, God said, must be closely and fearlessly examined. Much of it is inaccurate.

It is not our fault, God said. We did not, and could not, know any better. Yet now we can and do. And now we must act to *implement* what we know if we wish our species to not only be birthed, but to grow, to mature, to take its place in the Universe.

We must rewrite the story of Who We Are and Why We Are Here such that what we tell our children, and what they tell theirs, leads to a life radically different from our own, a life as it was intended to be lived.

As we begin in earnest, in 2012 and beyond, this wholesale rewriting and coauthoring process, I wonder if we can agree on some common objectives. Here are mine. How do these line up with yours? For my part, I'm hoping that our new story will be written in such a way that it will produce these outcomes:

1. An acceptance, at last, of the true identity of all humans as an aspect and an individuation of Divinity.

2. The embracing by more and more people— ultimately, millions—of the truth of the Oneness of all life and of humanity.

3. An understanding of why we are here upon the earth; a clarity as to the soul's agenda.

4. An end to abject poverty, to death by starvation,

and to mass exploitation of people and resources on the earth by those in positions of economic and/or political power.

5. An end to the systematic environmental destruction of the planet.

6. An end to the domination of our culture by an economic system rooted in competition above cooperation and in the continuing quest for economic growth.

7. An end to the endless struggle for Bigger/Better/ More.

8. An end to all limitations and discriminations holding people back—whether in housing, in the workplace . . . or in bed.

9. The providing, at last, of an opportunity—one that is truly equal—for all people to rise to the highest expression of Self.

This is the new world that I see—that I have been told by God it is now our opportunity to create. And here is the fastest way for us to accomplish these things: Step into our True Identity.

We are not simply advanced chemical expressions of physical life. We are spiritual expressions in physical form. We are, indeed, One with God. We are Divinity Expressed.

What we have not understood, the understanding of which will change everything, is that *we have been going after the wrong thing!* We have been trying to produce peace, prosperity, opportunity, happiness, and love for thousands of years. Yet our sights have been on the wrong goal—which is why we have not achieved it.

Our highest dreams above will be realized when we *self*-realize. They will come to pass when we come to know Who We Really Are. The knowing, the expressing, and the experiencing of our highest self is what would be most beneficial for us to be seeking. And now, at last, we know this. Thus, it is the shift *in what we are seeking* that is producing the Overhaul of Humanity.

As we seek this goal of self-realization, all of the other things for which we have so earnestly yearned and unsuccessfully struggled will begin to manifest in our lives automatically—even before we get to our goal, and even if we just start out in the right direction.

This is the great promise. We don't have to "get there," we just have to "head there." Or, as it has been much more eloquently put by another: *Seek ye first the Kingdom of God and all else will be added unto you.*

I know that you can accept and embrace this awareness. The very fact that you are reading this kind of book tells me so. I say, then, to you: *Thank you for joining the Welcoming Committee.* Let us usher in, together, our New Era.

Neale Donald Walsch *is a modern day spiritual messenger whose writings have been translated into thirty-seven languages, touching the lives of millions around the world. The author of twenty-eight books, seven of which have made the* New York Times *best seller list, his most recent writings include* When Everything Changes, Change Everything, *a combination of modern-day psychology and contemporary spirituality offering a pathway to peace in times of turmoil, and* The Storm Before the Calm, *which describes the presently occurring Overhaul of Humanity in specific terms and has served as the launching vehicle for www.TheGlobalConversation. com, an Internet platform for a planetary collaboration on a New Cultural Story for our species, coauthored by people from every walk of life in every nation on Earth.*

The Ancient Prophecy
of the Eagle and the Condor

By Lynne Twist

ONE OF THE GREATEST GIFTS I'VE RECEIVED IN THIS chapter of my life is the opportunity to work with indigenous people. I believe that at this special time in history, indigenous people have an enormous contribution to make to those of us from the modern world. They provide us with special access to the ancient past, which may be the most profound key we have to what I'll call "the deep future."

The indigenous people of the Amazon in particular are not caught, as we are, in what Father Thomas Berry calls "species isolation," which suggests that we as human beings have isolated ourselves so completely from all other species and from the natural world that we have gone into an almost hypnotic trance. This trance keeps us from understanding, relating to, and being deeply connected to the natural world around us. This hypnotic trance, he says, has us marching unconsciously towards our own demise. It is as if we are numb to the consequences of our individual and collective actions. Sadly, our ignorance is creating such profound danger that our only response is one of deeper denial.

The blessing of working with the indigenous peoples of the Amazon is that they are reaching out to us to help us wake up from the trance. Their cultures, which are still intact, hold the good of the community and all life as a higher ethical value than the good of the individual. These people are profoundly grounded in their relationship with all other species and the natural world. They do not live in the trance of materialism, and they do not suffer from an unconscious addiction to overconsumption; in fact, they do not even understand or have a relationship with this thing we call "money." In a special way, they serve as outside consultants to a culture that has lost its way. They can help us see the forest for the trees, and assist us to wake up and change our course before things become irreversible.

As a species we are no longer the subject of the evolutionary process; we have become the authors of it. This confers on us a profound responsibility that changes everything. It requires a level of consciousness, awareness, and spiritual depth greater than at any other time in history. Our partnership and relationship with indigenous people could be one of the most important keys to a successful and authentic rebirth of the human family at this deeply critical time in history. Their grounded relationship with the laws of the natural world, the true laws—laws that can never be negotiated on the Senate floor—keeps them centered in truth and integrity in a way that allows the authentic evolutionary process to powerfully come through them. This reality provides a powerful lesson to those of us from the modern world.

This is the time of the fulfillment of the Prophecy of the Eagle and Condor, which has been told for millennia by people in the Amazon and the Andes. The prophecy says this:

> At this time in history the "Eagle people"— which refers to the people who perceive life primarily through the mind—will have reached a zenith in their understanding and sophistication

in managing the power of the mind. They will even have invented tools to extend the capacity of the mind and will reach unprecedented material wealth. However, the "Eagle people" will be spiritually impoverished to their peril, and their very survival will be at risk. The "Condor people"— which refers to the branch of humanity that perceives life primarily through the wisdom of the heart and the five senses, and is grounded in the spirit world—are represented by the indigenous peoples of our planet. They will have reached a zenith in their understanding of the spirit world, according to their prophecies. They will have a profound relationship with all living kin, plants and animals, and will be remarkably sophisticated in their heart intelligence and intuition. At the same time, they will be materially impoverished in any encounter with the "Eagle people" and the material world, and their very survival will be at risk.

The prophecy says that just around this time in history, the beginning of the third millennium, the "Eagle people" and the "Condor people" will remember that they are each other, will join together, and fly in the same skies wing to wing, and the whole world will come back into balance.

The Prophecy of the Eagle and Condor is now coming true. It says that we will get through this transition, although difficult, and will arrive in a new era of balance and light. This hopeful prophecy is guiding indigenous people of the world and is a powerful beacon of light for all of us as we move toward the planetary birth of 2012 and beyond.

Lynne Twist—*global activist, consultant, speaker, and award-winning author of* The Soul of Money, *is* dedicated to global initiatives that create a sustainable future. As co-founder of the Pachamama Alliance (www.pachamama.org), she works with indigenous people of the Amazon and uses insights gained there to educate and inspire others to bring forth a thriving, just, and sustainable world. Twist is the founder/president of the Soul of Money Institute (www.soulofmoney.org), which has as its mission to educate, inspire, and empower people and organizations to align financial resources with what they value most. She has raised hundreds of millions of dollars to address humanity's most pressing issues, and has spoken to thousands in the business, nonprofit, and academic arenas. Twist has counseled people of high net worth in socially responsible giving and strategic philanthropy. Twist is a cocreator of the global media campaign, FOUR YEARS.GO (www.fouryearsgo.org) and is the winner of numerous prestigious awards, including Woman of Distinction from the United Nations.

A Shamanic Re-Membering of Universal Humanity

By Oscar Miro-Quesada

*"Only the grandeur of the natural world
can save our souls."*

—Thomas Berry

Never before has there been a greater need than now for a resonant field of soul-restorative shamanic consciousness in service to the emergence of a spiritually adept planetary culture. Founded upon sacred trust between humankind and the natural world, the embrace of shamanism as a life path leads to a generously unhindered beneficence of Self. The often-quoted Hopi expression "We are the ones we've been waiting for," is an irrefutable claim that we are naturally endowed with imaginative and physical resources for catalyzing the evolutionary ascension of a universal humanity. This is the living dream of our *Re-Membering*, the long-anticipated coming together after the separation.

We once moved through a wilderness where every plant, every rock, and every animal spoke to us, each embracing us in its song. Every moment was animated, charged with vitality and a sense of life-affirming wonder as humanity delighted in the ebb and flow of this fluid correspondence with the natural world. And so long as we were attentive and appreciative, we remained immersed in the abundant spirit of Mother Nature. We viscerally understood our Earth Mother's personal dream, the diverse expressions of her chosen involvement in cosmic eras and world cycles. Sensitive to the seen and unseen powers and forces of our soul-laden consciousness, we chose to establish deeply inviolate alliances for the greatest good of all. Being cautiously aware of the potentially disturbing impact that self-reflexive consciousness could have upon the seamless interdependence of life, we were careful not to let ourselves be subsumed by materialism. We kept alive the languages needed to cultivate this respectful relationship through ritual, song, dance, sacred pilgrimage, and the cocreative sustenance of earth-honoring community life. In these compassionate ways, people flourished and our children became elders who shared with every new generation the wisdom of the courtesies that allowed Earth and humanity to peacefully coexist in sacred trust. This is the story we must reclaim as our human birthright in order to assist the healthful flourishing of All Our Relations.

Any heartfelt practitioner of shamanism in the world today is deeply aware of the vital evolutionary role of this ancestral ecospiritual tradition. Shamanism has always honored the fact that all meaningful change occurs when the right not to change is first fully accepted. Indigenous culture is based on the understanding that people are not moved through persuasion; rather, people are moved through being aligned in purpose. Most traditional societies that value a soul-infused relationship in their dealings with the natural world remain deeply cognizant that communion and reconnection with the living earth always arouses the desire to act on its behalf. Those societies know that when you act on behalf of something greater than yourself, it acts through you with a power that is greater than your own. This truth is reason enough to justify inclusion of our Original Peoples ancestral wisdom within the dominant global institutions responsible for the social and economic well-being of humanity. I believe there is no more important contribution for the spiritualization of our *ethnosphere* and for providing sustenance for the evolutionary maturation of our planetary *noosphere*.

It is evident that humankind stands at a critical threshold regarding the species-wide survival of our Gaian biosphere. As the originator of the Pachakuti Mesa Tradition cross-cultural shamanism and visionary founder of the Heart of the Healer (THOTH) Foundation, I am committed to preserving and revitalizing time-proven indigenous lifeways. I hold a deep conviction that the nuanced gnosis and ritualized metaphor expressed in the mythic consciousness and ceremonial healing arts of our Ancient Ones are vital to our planetary survival. As we transition from an overly male-dominated social reality of progressive humanism, to a deeply feminine, relational embrace of eco-spiritual animism, today is the ideal liminal moment for shamanism to guide us forward in becoming *Homo universalis*—defined by Barbara Marx Hubbard as the evolutionary pinnacle of our human potential.

Whether we choose to associate "humanity's pay date" with Mayan 2012 prophecy, the Hopi teaching of the emergence of a Fifth World, or the Taripaypacha Pachakuti ("world transformation proceeding the prophesied Era of Re-Encounter") as called by the descendants of Peru's Inka, all of these references point to the due date when our debt will be maxed, and when no further credit from a depleted and overtaxed Nature will be extended to us. It is also the time when Nature's wake-up call, already sounding loudly, will reverberate through the psyche of humanity as a collective experience, as a shared frequency or resonance.

Having heeded a call from Great Spirit to serve as a catalyst for the emergence of such transformational resonance, I am convinced that awakening to this knowledge must be of the highest priority for humankind as a whole. In the words of poet John Keats, "Do you not see how necessary a World of Pains and troubles is to school an Intelligence and make it a soul? A Place where the heart must feel and suffer in a thousand diverse ways!" This excerpt is a perturbing reflection, an uncanny mirroring of this pivotal moment in our human evolution. Unless we choose a direction that honors a "making of soul," our world shall continue to intensify in suffering and pain.

Facing this unprecedented evolutionary choice as a self-reflexive planetary species, I'm reminded that of all world wisdom traditions born to ameliorate human suffering, shamanism is unequaled in matters of soul-making. The visionary insights revealed in shamanic cosmologies are beyond compare when applied to an understanding of our collective unconscious. The existence of shamanism is firmly rooted in the experiential understanding that the cosmos comprises a system of correspondences, notably between microcosm and macrocosm. It is impossible for any earnest practitioner of shamanism today to deny the phenomenology of a soul-animated cosmos in which all phenomena coexist in a balanced harmony of relatedness. I often refer to shamanic adepts as "walking theophanies." They are true visionary disciples of *Anima mundi* (the World Soul), who after many moons of deep apprenticeship in the sacred mysteries, became highly skilled at "growing corn and potatoes" (i.e., giving meaningful physical expression), while being guided by her soul-restorative imaginings. They have learned the sacred art of in-forming our world with healing grace and inspired beauty.

When performing artful rituals of reverence for nature befitting of seven generations, the past becomes present. When heartfelt shamanic ceremonies are reenacted at ancestrally venerated temple sites and pilgrimage destinations, all present are linked in visionary intention and soul-restorative action to all those that have gone before—to our shamanic ancestors and their inner sources of healing power and spiritual wisdom. That said, the Communion of Pioneering Souls—so often invoked through the loving consent of our dear sister Barbara—has been showering blessings on our planet through the intense force fields created by their spiritual practices since time immemorial. I trust all people on our good Earth shall soon be able to Tune-In to these same graces. *Aho Mitakuye Oyasin!*

Don Oscar Miro-Quesada *is a respected Peruvian kamasqa curandero, UN Observer to the Permanent Forum on Indigenous Issues, OAS Fellow in Ethnopsychology, originator of Pachakuti Mesa cross-cultural shamanism, and founder of the Heart of the Healer (THOTH) Foundation. Oscar has dedicated his life to the revitalization of ethnospiritual wisdom traditions as a way to restore sacred trust between humankind and the natural world. A popular international teacher and master ceremonialist, his work has been featured on CNN, Univision, A&E, and the Discovery Channel. Please visit www. heartofthehealer.org and www.mesaworks.com.*

Global Bifurcation:
The 2012 Decision Window

By Ervin Laszlo

IT HAS BEEN SAID THAT OUR GENERATION IS THE FIRST IN history that can decide whether it's the last in history. We need to add that our generation is also the first in history that can decide whether it will be the first generation of a *new* phase in history—a phase that could start at the end of 2012 as the emergence of a sustainable civilization birthed by the global emergency.

We have reached a watershed in our societal evolution. The sciences of systems tell us that when complex open systems—such as living organisms, and also ecologies and societies of organisms—approach a condition of critical instability, they face a moment of truth: they either transform, or break down. Humankind is approaching that moment of truth: a global bifurcation.

The following scenarios highlight the dimensions of the choice we face as we approach a point of bifurcation that could come as soon as the end of 2012.

1. The BAU (business as usual) Scenario

- There is no real change in the world in the way business is conducted, resources are exploited, and energy is produced. This leads on the one

hand to a worsening economic crisis characterized by frequent local financial crises leading to a
global crisis, and on the other to radical climate
change due to the accelerated warming of Earth's
atmosphere.

- In some regions of the world, global warming
  produces drought, in others devastating storms,
  and in many areas it leads to harvest failures. In
  coastal areas, vast tracts of productive land are
  flooded, together with cities, towns, and villages.
  Hundreds of millions are rendered homeless and
  face starvation.

- Massive waves of destitute migrants flow out of
  coastal regions and areas afflicted with lack of
  food and water—especially in Africa, Asia, and
  Latin America. As they move toward inland regions where the basic resources of life are more
  assured, these migrants overload the human and
  natural resources of the receiving countries and
  create conflict with the local populations. International relief efforts provide emergency supplies
  for thousands but are helpless when confronted
  with the needs of millions.

- In futile attempts to stem the tidal wave of destitute people, India builds a wall along its border
  with Bangladesh as does the United States along
  the Mexican border, and both Italy and Spain
  build walls to protect their northern regions from
  their overrun southern regions.

- The world's population fragments into states
  and populations intent on protecting themselves
  against masses of desperate people facing imminent famine and disease. The conflicts between
  these classes of people create unsustainable

stresses and strains in the structure of international relations. Social and economic integration groups and political alliances break apart. Relations break down between the United States and its southern neighbors, between the European Union and the Mediterranean countries, and amongst India and China and the hard-hit Southeast Asian states.

- Global military spending rises exponentially as governments attempt to protect their territories and reestablish a level of order. Strong-arm régimes come to power in the traditional hot-spots and local food- and water-wars erupt between states and populations pressed to the edge of physical survival.

- Terrorist groups, nuclear proliferators, narco-traffickers, and organized crime syndicates form alliances with unscrupulous entrepreneurs to sell arms, drugs, and essential goods at exorbitant prices. Governments target the terrorists and attack the countries suspected of harboring them, but more terrorists take the place of those that are rounded up and killed or imprisoned.

- Hawks and armaments lobbies press for the use of powerful weapons to defend the territories and interests of the better-off states. Regional wars fought initially with conventional arms escalate into wars conducted with weapons of mass destruction.

- The world's interdependent and now critically destabilized economic, financial, and political system collapses. The environment, its productive processes and vital heat balance impaired, is no longer capable of providing food and water for more than a fraction of the surviving populations. Chaos, disease, and violence engulfs peoples and countries both rich and poor.

There is, however, another scenario.

2. The TT (timely transformation) Scenario

- The experience of terrorism and war, together with rising poverty and the threats posed by a changing climate, trigger a widespread recognition that the time to change has come. In country after country, an initially small but soon rapidly growing nucleus of people pull together to confront the dangers of the global crisis and seize the opportunity it offers for change.

- The rise of popular movements for sustainability and peace leads to the election of political leaders who support economic cooperation and social-solidarity projects. Forward-looking states monitor the dangerous trends and provide financing for urgently needed economic, ecological, and humanitarian initiatives.

- Non-governmental organizations link up to undertake projects to revitalize regions ravaged by environmental degradation. Emergency funds are provided for countries and regions afflicted by drought, violent storms, coastal flooding, and failures of the harvest.

- Military budgets are reduced and in some states eliminated, and the resulting "peace-dividends" are assigned to increase the production of staple foods, safe water, basic supplies of energy, and essential sanitation and health services for the needy populations.

- Country after country shifts from fossil-fuel-based energy production to alternative fuels, reducing the release of greenhouse gases into the atmosphere and slowing the process of global warming. A globally networked renewable energy system comes on line, contributing to food production, providing energy for desalinizing and filtering seawater, and helping to lift marginalized populations from the vicious cycles of poverty.

- Leading businesses join the classical pursuit of profit and growth with the quest for social and ecological responsibility. On the initiative of enlightened managers, a voluntarily self-regulating social market economy is put in place, and the newly elected forward-looking political leaders give it their full support.

- As the new energy system and the self-regulating social market economy begins to function, access to economic activity and technical and financial resources becomes available to all countries and economies. Frustration, resentment, animosity, and distrust give way to a spirit of cooperation, liberating the spirit and enhancing the creativity of a new generation of locally active and globally thinking people. Humanity is on the way to a peaceful and sustainable and a diverse yet cooperative planet-wide civilization.

The choice between these scenarios has not yet been made. It is true that during the year 2012 we are still moving along the path of the BAU scenario. But the outlook is not hopeless. Among the most encouraging signs of the coming change is the awakening of millions, indeed hundreds if not thousands of millions, to the fact that BAU is not tenable and fundamental change is called for. One country after another has divested itself of traditional dictatorships, and people in country after country are taking action to destabilize the dominant institutions and authorities. The Arab Spring and the Occupy Wall Street movement are among the many indications of a global awakening. Such an awakening is needed to create an effective "worldshift"—and to create it in time. How much time is there? We know that the time is finite: as I previously indicated, when conditions in complex systems reach a critical phase, the system enters a bifurcation period—it either transforms, or breaks down.

To assess the size of the available decision-window, we must take into account both (1) the time by which current trends will have driven the system toward a critical phase, and (2) the cross-impacts and feedbacks that operate among the trends.

(i). The unfolding of individual trends. Time estimates of when individual system-destabilizing trends would reach points of criticality have been reduced from the end of the century to mid-century, and for some trends to the next few years.

For example, the sea level has been rising one and a half times faster than predicted in the IPCC's Third Assessment Report published in 2001. Current forecasts speak of a global sea-level rise that is more than double the 0.59 meter rise forecast by the Fourth Assessment Report.

Carbon dioxide emissions and global warming have likewise outpaced expectations. Since 2000, the growth-rate of emission has been greater than in any of the scenarios used by the IPCC in both the Third and Fourth Assessment Reports.

The warming of the atmosphere is progressing faster than expected as well. In the 1990s, forecasts spoke of an overall warming of maximum 3 degrees Celsius by the end of the century. Subsequently, the time-horizon for this level of increase was reduced to the middle of the century, and presently, some experts predict that it could occur within a decade. At the same time, the prediction for the maximum level of global warming rose from 3 to 6 degrees Celsius. The difference between 3 and 6 degrees is not negligible. A three degree warming would cause serious disruption in human life and economic activity, whereas a six degree warming would make nearly all of the planet unsuitable for food production and human habitation.

(ii) Feedbacks and cross-impacts. Most predictions of the time by which trends would reach a point of criticality take only the given trend into consideration—for example, global warming and attendant climate change; water quality and availability; food production and self-reliance; urban viability, poverty, and population pressure; air quality and minimal health standards, among others. They fail to consider the possibility that criticality in one trend could accelerate the coming of criticality in the others. In point of fact, there are multiple feedbacks and cross-impacts among the system-threatening global trends in regard to conditions both in the biosphere and in the human world.

With respect to the biosphere, all the trends that affect human life and well-being also impact the cycles that maintain the planet's ecology within the range where it can support seven billion humans. This is the case in regard to the global water and the global carbon cycle: the alteration of these cycles by any one trend affects the way the other trends unfold. For example, an increase of carbon dioxide in the atmosphere leads to global warming and that affects rainfall and the growth of forests. This, in turn, reduces the biosphere's carbon absorption capacity. Feedbacks are also conveyed by air and ocean currents. Warmer water in the oceans triggers hurricanes and other violent storms and alters the course of major ocean currents, such as the Gulf and the Humboldt.

And that effect, in turn, triggers further changes in the climate. These cross-impacts drive toward conditions where only a fragment of the currently seven billion humans on Earth could get access to sufficient clean water, breathable air, and productive soil sufficient to enable even a bare subsistence.

Such positive feedbacks also obtain between ecological and societal trends. Here are several examples:

- The warming of the atmosphere produces prolonged drought in some areas and coastal flooding in others. Starving and homeless masses are impelled to migrate from the highly impacted areas to less hard-hit regions, creating critical conditions in the receiving regions as well.

- A drop in the quality of the air in urban and industrial megacomplexes below the minimum required for health creates a breakdown in public health, with epidemics spreading to vast areas.

- A breakdown of the financial system impacts not only on banks and stock markets but interferes with industrial output and trade, creating critical conditions first of all for the world's least developed economies and populations.

As I have shown in previous books, these and related cross-impacts among the currently accelerating system-threatening trends reduce the size of the available decision-window. This window may close at the end of 2012, within a year from the time of writing at the end of 2011. This would coincide with the famous Mayan, Hopi, and astrological prophesies that predict a major phase-change at that time in the human world. The likely closing of the decision-window does not mean that a new civilization *will* then take shape; it only indicates that, if humanity is to survive, a new civilization *must* take shape in order for humanity to avoid a global bifurcation event. There are no alternatives to using the system-transforming potential of the global emergency to initiate a process of global emergence. The widespread expectation of a major transformation at the end of 2012 is a perfect and unique occasion to begin the process of emergence.

Ervin Laszlo is founder and president of the Club of Budapest, chancellor of the Giordano Bruno GlobalShift University, founder of the General Evolution Research Group, fellow of the World Academy of Arts and Sciences, member of the Hungarian Academy of Science and the International Academy of Philosophy of Science, senator of the International Medici Academy, and editor of the international periodical World Futures: The Journal of Global Education. *He has a PhD from the Sorbonne and is the recipient of honorary PhD's from the United States, Canada, Finland, and Hungary. Formerly a professor of philosophy, systems science, and futures studies in various universities in the United States, Europe, and the Far East, he now lectures worldwide. Laszlo received the Peace Prize of Japan, the Goi Award in 2002, the International Mandir of Peace Prize in Assisi in 2005, the Conacreis Holistic Culture Prize in 2009, and was nominated for the Nobel Peace Prize in 2004 and 2005. He is the author or coauthor of fifty-four books translated into as many as twenty-three languages, and serves as editor of another thirty volumes in addition to a four-volume World Encyclopedia of Peace. He lives in the hills of Tuscany.*

The Birth of a Global Citizenry:
Fantasy, or Future Reality?

By Michael Bernard Beckwith

As you read these words, a radical change in humanity's movement towards global solidarity is taking root. The transformation of an egocentric model of "me and mine" into a world-centric mindset of "we and ours" is the vessel that accommodates such a revolution of values, creating space for the emergence of a global citizenry. Birthing this profound sense of stewardship begins within the consciousness of each individual, because *how we govern our individual life determines the character of international relations on our planet.* As Carl Jung summed it up, "In the history of the collective as in the history of the individual, everything depends on the development of the consciousness." It is very encouraging that in today's scientific and spiritual communities consciousness is accepted as an undeniable component of the human being.

It is also true that when a collective consciousness of greed, racism, violence, and war floods the international bloodstream, it breaks out as toxic ignorance upsetting the organic balance of the whole, causing wisdom, love, peace, and justice to flounder. As the Indian sage Krishnamurti points out, "The inward strife projected outwardly becomes the world chaos. After all, war is the spectacular result of our everyday life. The way of peace is simple. It is the way of truth and love. It starts with the individual himself. To go far, one must begin near. The first actions are within. The sources of peace are not outside us, and the heart of man is in his own keeping." As more and more individuals evolve in consciousness, so will there be a corresponding realization of their oneness with all existence.

Technology Has Restructured the World into a Neighborhood

There you are, sitting in your living room watching a great ball game when all at once you hear, "We interrupt this program with breaking news . . . ," or a Facebook or Twitter message you just received urges you to protest man's expressions of inhumanity to man and other injustices. This is technology at its best: a vehicle of social synergy, turning the world into a neighborhood in ways that were previously unimaginable. Immediate access to world events through tightly interconnected information systems allows individuals to press world leaders in government, human rights, science, economics, law, the environment, philosophy, and spirituality to take action on local and international issues and specific policies.

Architects of Global Change

I consider all human beings to be world citizens. Socrates put it out there when he declared, "I am not Greek, or even Athenian. I am a citizen of the world." Mohandas K. Gandhi, Dr. Martin Luther King Jr., and Nelson Mandela revolutionized their societies through their inner realization of this truth. They also taught us that there is no separation between our political, social, and spiritual endeavors—all are to be governed by the truth that we are indeed one interdependent global family cocreating the destiny of our planet.

You might ask whether it is realistic to entrust humanity to be architects of global change. Yes, it is, because when enough individuals adopt the possibility of an ethical form of world governance as not being naive or utopian, we will begin to actualize what is endeavoring to birth itself on the planet. Transcendent wisdom will then emerge, such as appears in quantum physicist's John Hagelin's book, *Manual for a Perfect Government*: ". . . the experience of pure consciousness corresponds to the direct subjective experience of the unified field of all the laws of nature at the foundation of the physical universe. The influence of positivity and coherence generated by such group practice thus represents an actual physical influence of peace that in magnitude is more powerful than any previous defensive technology. If, according to the UNESCO Charter, 'War begins in the minds of men,' then it can easily end in the far more fundamental experience of pure consciousness which underlies and unites us all."

Global solidarity cannot be created by force; it must sprout in the fertile soil of individual consciousness, become embodied, and then express itself through corresponding action. "All the religions and all the peoples of the world are undergoing the most radical, far-reaching, and challenging transformation in history," wrote the late Ewert Cousins, Fordham Professor of Theology Emeritus. "Forces, which have been at work for centuries, have in our day reached a crescendo that has the power to draw the human race into a global network." The evolutionary thrust of the universe is calling for each of us to expand in consciousness so that we may consciously participate in birthing a new society grounded in the realization of oneness that connects human beings across space and time.

The Power within a Question

One of our most cherished rights and processes is to question. Throughout human history, posing questions has contributed towards advances in science, religion, philosophy, cosmology, and spirituality, and has led to major inventions. Socrates's typical opening of a philosophical dialogue was to raise questions such as, "What is justice?" Inquiry invites new possibilities to emerge. Honest reflection gives rise to the big questions of our individual existence, and nonjudgmental observation of our responses contributes to both individual and collective awakening. When we ask a question that comes from our depths, our capacity to listen and receive a response with the inner ear of intuition is expanded. In that feeling tone, I invite you to commit the gift of your consciousness, talents, and skills to the campaign for Birth 2012. It is my hope that the following questions will support you in identifying where you stand in the continuum of birthing a consciousness of a global citizenry on the planet and amplifying the future evolution of our shared earth and of all sentient beings:

Do I believe in the possibility of an evolutionary shift that has the potential to be greater than anything the world has experienced?

What does the world I want to live in look like?

What qualities must I cultivate to contribute to the world I want to see?

What qualities must I release to contribute to the world I want to see?

Do I believe that humanity's collective vision and agreement can create a world that works for everyone?

How can I bring my life in sync with the fundamental urge of the universe to evolve in a progressive way?

Michael Bernard Beckwith is the founder of the Agape International Spiritual Center in Los Angeles. He is a sought-after speaker, meditation teacher, retreat facilitator, and originator of the Life Visioning Process™ (LVP). Beckwith is the author of Life Visioning, Spiritual Liberation: Fulfilling Your Soul's Potential, The Answer Is You, Forty Day Mind Fast Soul Feast, Inspirations of the Heart, *and* A Manifesto of Peace. *He has appeared on* The Oprah Winfrey Show, Larry King Live, Tavis Smiley, *in his own PBS special,* The Answer Is You, *and can be heard on his weekly radio broadcast on KPFK. Visit him at www.agapelive.com.*

Dear Planetary Family

By Ashok K. Gangadean

[For an explanation of special markings and usages,
see the notes at the end of this essay. – Ed.]

WELCOME TO ((PRESENCE)). WELCOME ((HOME)).
OUR arrival in ((Presence)) is a climax of our great evolutionary journey over millennia and through the ages. And this miraculous moment of shift has been pioneered and prepared by our great Evolutionary Elders, our spiritual, enlightenment, and wisdom teachers across our planetary home. Our diverse evolutionary pioneers such as Abraham, Buddha, Socrates, Lao Tzu, Moses, Krishna, Jesus, Mohammed, countless Sophias who embody this wisdom, and many, many others through the ages have been calling us to make a profound evolutionary shift in our form of life for the sake of the maturation of our species. But the full power of their evolutionary call, which itself has been maturing over the centuries, has reached a new and unprecedented threshold—a global shift moment—where we can encounter the evolved global power of their consensus teaching as never before.

The teachings of our Evolutionary Elders naturally remained rather localized in the diverse cultural languages in which they were articulated, encountered, and received. But a great evolutionary lesson of the ages is

that if and when we stand back from our more localized cultural lens and dilate our heart-minds into a more
expansive and evolved global lens, we can begin to see
striking evolutionary patterns and witness a global consensus emergent from our diverse enlightened teachers.
When we dilate our minds, allow the power of our script
to ignite and enter this expanded global space, we are
able to connect the hitherto scattered "dots," scattered
"scriptures," teachings, narratives—and astounding
patterns come into relief that could not be clearly seen
before. Through this evolutionary shift to the global
lens and global dilated consciousness, we may finally see
clearly that our diverse enlightened teachers through the
ages are in global consensus and our treasured scriptures
concur in calling our human family to this Sacred Space
of ((Presence)).

Whether in the teachings of Jesus or Buddha or
Krishna, to focus for a moment on selected preeminent
Evolutionary Elders, it becomes clear that the essence of
their call to humanity is to let go of dysfunctional "ego-
mental" patterns of consciousness and culture-making
and make a dimensional shift to a global, integral, holistic, and dialogic pattern of life, culture, and experience.
There is a striking consensus that ego-mental "minding" with its "monocentric" level of script or language
coproduces abysmal fragmentation, polarization, objec-
tification, and alienation that spawns the diverse range of
human dysfunctions and pathologies of life that we now
see across our planet.

The chronic and endemic breakdowns in relations
and communications across diverse borders—leading
to holocausts, genocides, ethnic cleansing, racism, sex-
ism, wars, terrorism, crusades, and wide-ranging forms
of violence—are found to be directly traceable to the
fragmenting and dis-integral mental patterns of life and
culture-making that issue from ego-mental minding and
scripting. Indeed, the countless local and global crises

faced by humanity on a planetary scale today can be directly traced to the continued dominance of ego-mental patterns of living.

This ego-mental stage of our human development—self-making, culture-making, world-making—remains severed from the Primal Source, the Holistic Unified Field of Reality that flows in boundless ((Presence)). These enlightened teachers, each in their own unique way, were focusing their diagnostic genius to help humanity see that remaining lodged in such ego-mental patterns of life generates abysmal human suffering—existential pathologies of all kinds—and is a primary barrier to our healthful maturation as whole persons in sustainable, awakened, and compassionate cultures. We urgently need to mature into this global awakening to experience this remarkable enlightenment consensus of our Evolutionary Elders. This distilled wisdom focuses our attention as never before on the pervasive depth of ego-mental patterns of life and culture as well as on the magnitude of the required dimensional shift to liberated life in our evolutionary crossing into ((Presence)).

Our individual and collective shift into this Field of ((Presence)) lifts us into human flourishing at all levels. Our Evolutionary Elders narrated in diverse ways that there is and must be a Primal Infinite Originating Field that is the ever-present Source of all existence, life, culture, experience—the Field of Reality itself. Whether or not this ((First Energy Field)) is called "Tao" or "Aum" or "Yahweh" or "Christ" or "Buddha Nature" or "Brahman" or "Allah" or the "Unified Field" of Science, it becomes stunningly clear through the ((Global Lens)) that this ((Primal Force)) is the moving cause and source of all evolution. This ((Infinite First)) is the global moving force of all existence and the primary telos or arrival locus of all events and developments in the universe. The emergence of this ((Logos)), and our arrival in ((Presence)), is thus the leading headline event of all evolutionary stories. This locus is the Infinite Space of ((Presence)).

Our evolutionary journey into this ((Presence)) arrives at the Energy Field of Infinite ((Connectivity)) and ((Cocreative Flow)). This Field of ((Presence)), our global teachers have rightly insisted, is nothing less than the monumental dimensional shift from our /ego-mental/ stage of development to our present maturation into the holistic, integral, and dialogical space of flourishing and compassionate life. Buddha's great awakening and his teaching of Four Noble (Global) Truths, for example, focused precisely on this dimensional shift from /ego-mental/life—which produces existential suffering and fragmentation—into the Nirvanic Field of ((Emptiness)) of the full flourishing of Buddha Nature where humans mature into the flow of compassion, well being, and happiness. In our dilated ((Global Lens)) we can now see that Buddha's ((Emptiness)) is ((Presence))—the technology of Being Here Now.

Buddha urges humanity to recognize the pathological suffering that comes from /ego-mental/ life and teaches us the therapeutic pathways to rehabilitate our patterns of minding the Field of ((Buddha Energy)), which is the Sacred Space of ((Presence)). We will see in a moment that this great shift from /ego-mental/ life into the mindful life of ((Presence)) is a dimensional shift and comes now with our crossing into an evolved form of ((Script)) an ((Enlightened Literacy)) and our maturation into our ((Global Lens)).

But let's take a moment as we now arrive in ((Presence)) to see that this is the essence of Jesus's call to humanity to let go of the life of /sin/ and cross into the rebirth of ((Christ Consciousness)). The teachings of ((Jesus)) had to evolve and mature over the centuries to be truly appreciated in their full ((Global Gospel Power)). ((Jesus)) spoke to us in strange ways—as the ((Logos in the Flesh)). He was the ((Living Script of Logos)) and he insisted that the ((Law of Love)) must be lived and embodied in the ((heart-mind)). The life and sacrifice of Jesus is precisely this call to our evolutionary shift and maturation to true ((Human Form)). He lived and embodied this dimensional shift to the ((Script of Presence)). So here, too, as we arrive in ((Presence)), we can see that the depth of ((Christ Consciousness)) meets the Energy field of ((Compassionate Buddha)) in the ((Life of Presence)). Here we find boundless Diversity in the Space of Infinite Unity.

With these two striking examples we can perhaps begin to see that our great evolutionary journey and shift is a rite of passage of "dimensional" proportions; it is a dimensional shift from an /ego-mental/ stage of evolution to the ((Living Script of Presence)). So important is this evolutionary shift to a higher form of ((Script)) of ((Life)) of ((Human Species Maturation)), that we urgently need ((script markers)) to mark and bring into the open this all-important, life-and-death, evolutionary shift from /life/ to ((Life)). And we use these "evolutionary, dimensional shift markers" to complete our journey from /ego-mental culture/ to awakened mindful ((Life)) in the Sacred Space of ((Presence)).

In this sense, the heart of our evolutionary journey and the ((shift)) we now celebrate in our unprecedented arrival in ((Presence)) is our shift from /ego sapiens/ to ((LogoSapiens)), from /ego pillars/ to ((Buddhaflies)). The great ((shift)) we celebrate now is our shift from /life/ to ((Life)), from /ego human/ to ((Logos Beings)), that is, to mature morally awakened ((Persons)). We mature from /script/ to ((Script)), from /ego lens/ to ((Global Lens)) as we enter ((Presence)), the Space of ((Global Enlightenment)). This evolutionary maturation to ((Holistic Script)) is the living ((Literacy)) of the awakened ((Global cultures)). We celebrate in this arrival in ((Presence)) the democratization of ((Enlightenment))—that is, awakened ((rational life)).

Our arrival now in ((Presence)) is a birthright for our entire human family. ((Enlightenment)) is not reserved for a select, elite few while the rest of humanity is left behind. We humans are born for ((Enlightenment)) and this is nothing other than our evolutionary journey into ((rational life)). We are ((rational beings)), ((logosapiens)), and our arrival together now into the ((life of presence)) is our individual and collective ((co-enlightenment)). Thus, ((Enlightenment)) is not a "luxury," an "extra" and "utopian bonus" that we can't afford to pursue, but is now an absolute ((necessity)) that we cannot afford to ignore. We must now ((awaken)) or sink more deeply into the evolutionary crises facing us on all sides.

This great ((shift)) is also at the center of the teachings of Lord Krishna in the Bhagavad Gita. This third prominent model of our great ((evolutionary shift)) shines through the deep dialogue between Krishna and Arjuna, who acts as the stand-in for the /ego-based/ human who is lodged in /ego-mental culture/. Krishna leads /Arjuna/ in this deep existential and evolutionary therapy to become aware of his /ego-mental/ life and to enter the higher ((literacy)) of ((Yoga Science and Technology)): the multiple alternative pathways into the ((Script of Aum)), as Arjuna matures into his higher ((Self)), to ((Arjuna)) who enters the ((Yoga Zone)), to ((Be Here Now)) in the sacred space of ((Presence)). Here we see that the art-science of ((Yoga)) is the quieting of the /ego-mental mind/ and patterns of /life/ and enables us to make the evolutionary shift into the higher non-dual, integral or ((holistic literacy)) of ((Integral Life)). Gandhi's life is a model of this evolutionary shift to nonviolent, compassionate, integral living.

We can find striking models and examples of this evolutionary ((shift)) across the planet and through the ages. Every pulse of existence is situated in the Energy Field of ((Presence)). All our /ego-mental/ cultures are situated within this ((Infinite Field)) and could not exist apart from ((Presence)). And now that we are sharing this long emerging and hitherto missing ((Story)), we can see the truly astounding findings of ((Global Wisdom)) through our dilated ((Global Lens)) and ((Holistic Script)). Perhaps one of the most striking disclosures is that /ego-mental/ minding and scripting and living is a primary generative cause of human existential pathologies and dysfunctions.

Our level of /scripting/ and /minding/ produces human suffering and living pathologies at the individual and cultural levels. And in light of this ((Global Evolutionary Script)), it is truly remarkable that despite the teachings of our Evolutionary Elders, urging humanity to make this ((shift)) from the /I/>>>/It/ mind space to the ((I <===> Thou)) form of ((Life)), nevertheless our human cultures appear to be still lodged chronically within the dysfunctional and harmful /ego-mental/ patterns of self-making, world-making, and culture-making.

This is why our arrival together in ((Presence)) is an occasion of wondrous celebration. Our human family crosses the great evolutionary divide—the dimensional shift—from /culture/ to ((Culture)), wherein we blossom as full ((Humans)), into the maturation of our ((Species)) in becoming ((Persons)). Now we enter the ((I <===> Thou)) mindful literacy of sacred life in ((deep dialogue)). We rise together in the ((global space)) wherein ((deep democracy)) flows in awakened ((moral consciousness)). This evolutionary shift opens deeper dimensions of ((science)) and the encounter with ((Nature)).

This ((Life in Presence)) is the sacred space wherein we finally have the literacy and rational competence to honor ((diversity)) whilst still within the boundless space of ((Unity)), ((Y Pluribus Unum)). Now ((Individuals)) can celebrate our natural inner multiplicity without inner fragmentation and polarization and disintegration. With this literacy of ((Presence)), we can find personal ((Integrity)) and ((Inner Peace)). Our Interpersonal relations can flow in ((deep dialogue)) across all borders. We can celebrate the sacred ((diversity)) of our multiple ((religious worlds)) and ((scriptures)) in the ((Global Spirituality)) of ((Presence)). And we may now flourish together as a human family sharing our ((Sacred Earth)).

Welcome to ((Presence)). Welcome ((Home)).

Notes on Special Usages and Markings

Definition of "script":

The word "script" evokes the meanings of "language," "narrative," and "scripture." It is now vital to recognize that our language, or what I prefer to call "script," encodes our evolutionary development and dimension of consciousness. Our great spiritual traditions concur that in the ((beginning)) is the ((word)), and this is primal, infinite script. And the phrase "Word of God" is ((scripture)). Thus, the /ego-mental/ "script" is a different evolutionary dimension from the more evolved ((script)) of ((logos))—the ((script of presence)).

Use of special markings:

One of the astounding findings of the ages is that the deepest impulse in cultural evolution across the planet is to cross over, through a dimensional shift, from the ego-mental stage of literacy to the awakened holistic script of the ((Unified field of Logosophia)), or what I call the shift into ((Presence)). One face of this startling finding in our evolutionary journey is the introduction of markers to remind us at all times when we are within the /ego-mental/ stage of our evolutionary development and when we have crossed into ((Presence)) and thus entered the awakened ((script)) of the ((logosphere)). The ego-mental mind does not have direct access to this ((awakened script)), spoken of and embodied by ((Jesus, Buddha, and Krishna)), for example. This evolved ((script of Presence)) is a ((living script)). In short, then, it may be said that our evolutionary journey through the ages is from /life/ to ((life)), /culture/ to ((culture)), /ego sapien/ to ((Logo-sapien)). As widely diverse as our worldviews, cultures, religions, ideologies may be, it is vital to realize that they nevertheless exist in the same dimensional boat. And my use of the "/x/" marker brings this stunning fact into the open. Similarly, through our dilated ((holistic lens)) it becomes evident that our diverse wisdom and spiritual teachings are calling our human family to mature and shift into the awakened ((dimension of presence)), and the "((x))" marker brings this life-and-death fact into the open.

Ashok K. Gangadean is Margaret Gest Professor of Global Philosophy at Haverford College where he has taught for the past forty-four years. Throughout his career he has focused on clarifying the fundamental common ground across widely diverse worldviews and has sought to expand philosophy and cultural life into a wider global context. He is founder-director of the Global Dialogue Institute, which has developed effective methods of Deep Dialogue for renovating cultural life. His forthcoming book is Awakening Global Enlightenment. *A six-CD audio version of this book recently appeared with Sounds True. Ashok is also coconvenor of the World Commission on Global Consciousness and Spirituality, which brings leading and emerging world leaders together in deep dialogue to help articulate global wisdom, vision, and values in addressing the most pressing concerns and crises on a global scale. He is also cochair of the World Wisdom Council. His most recent book,* Meditations of Global First Philosophy: Quest for the Missing Grammar of Logos (SUNY Press, 2008) *introduces new dimensions of ((global reason and enlightenment)). His website is:* www.awakeningmind.org.

Coming Together to Coauthor a New Story

By Dot Maver

WE ARE—RIGHT NOW—IN THE MIDST OF THE PAIN AND exhilaration of birthing a new humanity, a new culture, a new civilization, a new living expression of our world and all of its wonders and challenges. What a time to be alive, to be participating in and creating a whole fresh phase of life for our planet.

Yes, we are facing a huge residue of old and outdated thinking, reacting, and acting; yet, the old ways have served to bring us to this exciting and unprecedented moment in our shared journey towards a future whose possibilities we are only beginning to imagine. Our task is to keep imagining, to stay open to the new potential and spend as little energy as possible in reacting to all that must inevitably pass in the face of the potency of what is emerging.

Humanity stands on a threshold—a threshold as significant as any in recorded history. It could be compared to the European Dark Ages in this respect. At that darkest moment of fear, oppression, confusion, and chaos, could we have known that we were just a few steps away from a renaissance? The human species is the only one with the capacity to create form, and to produce color and sound in harmonious relation—the path of beauty—and to do so even in the darkest of times. Five centuries later, do we have the will to spark a new renaissance—on a planetary scale? Are we willing to take responsibility to do so?

Watching the recent WeDay (WeDay.com) broadcast about thousands of youth choosing to make a difference, telling their stories and making a commitment to change the world, inspires confidence that, yes, the next generation is already taking on this responsibility. These young people along with the adults of our generation are the transition team taking shared responsibility for the shift into a culture of peace and right relationship.

Humanity is experiencing an expansion of consciousness. We are understanding our place in the greater whole and that we are responsible for playing a wise part in this ecosystem called Earth. If we want a different future, we need a different story and we, each one of us, are the storytellers.

At the heart of the new story is the science of right human relationships in a culture of peace—relationships with self, others, and the world around us. The Earth Charter, a document created by people from all over the world, addresses humanity's relationship with one another and Earth as a whole system, stating, "Peace is the wholeness created by right relationships with oneself, other persons, other cultures, other life, Earth, and the larger whole of which all are a part."

A good example of organic coauthoring of the emergent new story is the Occupy Wall Street (OWS) movement and its replications in cities all across the United States and around the world. OWS is a manifestation of what Buckminster Fuller suggests when he states, "You never change things by fighting the existing reality. To change something, build a new model that makes the existing model obsolete." So, as we experience an all-systems breakdown, we are clearly, at the same time, in the midst of an all-systems breakthrough.

And although the new forms are still taking shape and thus not yet clearly visible, *the new story entails a whole-systems approach.* The message of whole-systems thinking is at the heart of the OWS movement: we cannot do "business as usual" in our society, and every voice counts. Further, certain principles that are foundational to a transformed society— nonviolence and cooperation—are the central tenets.

The new story is one of right relationship in a whole-systems understanding along with a focus on beauty and culture. This story is reflected through the Pax Cultura symbol on the Roerich Banner of Peace. On April 15, 1935, at the White House in Washington DC, President Franklin D. Roosevelt oversaw the signing of the Treaty for the Protection of Artistic and Scientific Institutions and Historic Monuments, also known as the Roerich Pact. In concept similar to the use of the Red Cross symbol in wartime, this pact, signed by the United States and twenty Latin American countries, calls for the Banner of Peace to be the universal symbol that flies over all cultural institutions (schools, museums, libraries, etc.) in times of peace and war, in order to make certain that the culture of all peoples would be protected and preserved. The Banner of Peace (see Figure 3 below) is an initiating impulse in the spirit of a new, *global*, renaissance.

Figure 3

In the Banner of Peace symbol, the outer circle represents culture— humanity's culture. The three inner circles represent a synthesis of science, religion and the arts. When we learn to appreciate and celebrate one another's cultures, humanity shifts to living in Pax Cultura.

The Russian philosopher and painter Nicholas Roerich, designer of the Banner of Peace, said, "This sign, unfurled over all treasures of human genius, will say: Here are guarded the treasures of all [hu]mankind, here above all petty divisions, above illusory frontiers of enmity and hatred, is towering the fiery stronghold of love, labour and all-moving creation." Culture is the great unifier; the artisans and creators remind us daily of our essential goodness and that beauty plays a unique and significant role in life.

The very society we have created is undergoing radical transformation—an "extreme makeover." As we create the new story, may we have the will, wisdom, and creative intelligence to take the best from the past and weave it through into the day-to-day workings of our life together as a human family.

Each one of us has a unique contribution to make in this world. I realized years ago that no matter what job I am "doing," I am in fact always striving to inspire cooperation on behalf of the common good. Take a quiet moment of deep reflection. What is your unique contribution to this planetary shift?

When major change happens in life, our tendency is to dig in our heels and resist. In these times, may we have the wisdom, willingness, and courage to let go and go with the flow of the emergence of the new story. There is no greater moment of probability for transformation than right now.

Dorothy J. Maver, PhD, is an educator and peacebuilder whose keynote is inspiring cooperation on behalf of the common good. She is a founder and president of the National Peace Academy, USA; a founder of the Global Alliance for Ministries and Infrastructures for Peace; serves as executive director of the River Phoenix Center for Peacebuilding; and helps coordinate Push4Peace.org. Maver formerly served as executive director of the Peace Alliance and Campaign for a US Department of Peace, and prior to that was the national campaign manager for Kucinich for President 2004. Dr. Maver is the creator of a technique, The Maver Method: Secrets of Softball Hitting Success, and coauthor of Conscious Education: The Bridge to Freedom, *and serves on the board of directors at the Nicholas Roerich Museum in New York City.*

The Birth of the Peace Child

By James O'Dea

ONCE AND FOR ALL, LET'S DISSOLVE THE MYTH OF THE so-called average human being. You as a human being are a unique creation. No one has your qualities. No one has your experience. Thus, no person on the face of Earth can have your perspective on the world.

Your unique experience is gold in our collective evolutionary process. Your learning is reflected in the universal field of all experience and in the great mirror of nature. Be assured that you live a personal life, but you are also a hologram of the entire evolutionary process and a vital part of life's indestructible archive. Everything you experience is sifted for its meaning and everything has purpose in informing the emergent design of our collective future.

For each one of us, our experience in life is a steep hill that no one else, only we, get to climb. From each sacred hill of personal experience we get to look down on all that we have learned, what insights we have gained, and the wisdom we may have to share. But we can turn and see that the hills we stand on are foothills to the very great mountain of humanity's collective experience. When we climb that greater mountain we see the inheritance of our collective effort: our fumbling, tumbling, and brilliant advances. It is to this mountain we must go if we are to see the whole story.

Up there, you can see all the patterns of connection that weave so many hills, valleys, fields, and streams into one landscape. Up there, what lies behind and what lies ahead is part of one vast design.

My personal foothill was to climb a path of suffering and celebration. I was conceived on the eve of my sister's death as she moved toward her eleventh birthday. Like a secret, I was hidden in my mother's womb as she mourned so deeply the loss of her beautiful daughter. By the time she realized she was pregnant, her suffering was being written into my cellular memory and I was forming as Life's answer to the pain of her loss. Sure enough, when I was born my mother gave the signal that it was time to celebrate the new life.

Each of our lives is a coded fractal of humanity's larger story. In my case, the codes were about the movement from loss to recovery, from suffering to celebration, and from wounding to healing. My life has taken me deep into these themes. I have been taken to witness brutality and war, carnage and cruelty. For many years I woke up every day to work on rescuing people from the torture slab or to intervene to end rampant human rights abuses across the planet. But I was called to go even deeper and answer the question, "How do we get so wounded that we can do such terrible things to each other? How can we heal those wounds?"

I spent time dialoguing with victims of torture and abuse, survivors of genocide and massacres. I sat in circle with both perpetrators and victims, always looking for where the wounding began. This was my journey up the mountain of our collective experience of suffering. I needed perspective on how these wounds of soul and psyche get transferred from generation to generation; how they move inside cultures; how they become framed as belief systems about "the other" and then harden into economic and political structures. As I confronted the dense shadows of these realities, I began to see something that arrested my attention even more than the violence that seemed endless—I began to see how humans heal from these wounds.

Nothing prepared me for the awe that I experienced upon meeting people who had forgiven their torturers or even forgiven those who had murdered family members in the frenzy of ethnic violence. Nothing prepared me for the revelatory experience of the sacred in meeting those who perpetrated human rights abuses and cruelty only to become exemplars of creative atonement and community reconciliation. It was as if I was called up the mountain to see what needs to be seen in this conflicted hour of humanity's unfolding narrative.

There, standing in the midst of terror and trauma, was a human being whose nature had evolved beyond vengeance and violently reactive punishment. At first I was inclined to perceive this expression of humanity as a miraculous anomaly. But the more my work took me to the shattered places of the world, the more I saw this healing emerge. I saw it in luminous children and wise elders who lived peacefully on the front lines of violence. I saw it in bereaved families who reached across the divide to comfort each other in the mutuality of their pain. I observed it in survivors of genocide who dedicated themselves to healing the wounds of ethnic hatred. I saw it in the example of abusers who experienced the transformative light of truth, reconciliation, and forgiveness.

Now I understand that the Universe was calling me to witness the birth of a new humanity. I saw that these healing capacities were coming into the world when we needed them most.

I see now how the underlying weave of this evolving capacity is supported by new science, which affirms that our truest well-being comes from healing relationships, from love, empathy, gratefulness, and forgiveness. I see also how accelerating global connectivity breaks down barriers and confronts the myth of separation and cultural superiority. I understand how any form of domination is doomed to failure, for this is a story about the whole healing the whole. To heal, in fact, means to restore wholeness.

We are at the dawn of a whole-system shift as we witness this early immune response to the viral challenges of greed and manipulation.

This is a shift in which conscience will be reignited in the consciousness awakening across the entire field of humanity—a conscience that no longer needs the wrong to prove the right, and whose luminous inclusiveness affirms that all our wounding can be healed. It is a conscience whose moral compass points to compassionate justice and social order based upon the freedom to create and express the deep bonds of our connection and interdependence.

And so, I am coming down from the mountain with an inexpressible gratitude and a song in my heart. For I wish to look into your eyes and your eyes and your eyes. I want to see if you can hear, as I do, the Great Mother say, "Wipe away your tears. I have conceived the peace child. I have given birth to a race of healers. I have given birth to a new human race. Behold and celebrate this new Earth tribe that came through a path of suffering and loss to find the knowledge that can end all wounding, envy, and hatred. Celebrate, for the bitter and the sweet have been compounded into a healing balm of unitary consciousness that is destined to create a new planetary civilization. And the hallmark of its civility will be joy."

James O'Dea is a renowned figure in international social healing who has conducted healing and reconciliation dialogues for twenty years. He is currently the codirector of the Social Healing Project, whose work has led him to Rwanda, Israel/Palestine, and Northern Ireland. He also facilitates Peace Ambassador Training hosted by the Shift Network. O'Dea is on the extended faculty of the Institute of Noetic Sciences and is its immediate past president. The former Washington, DC, office director of Amnesty International and CEO of the Seva Foundation, O'Dea is a member of the Evolutionary Leaders Group founded by Deepak Chopra. His most recent book, Creative Stress, *was featured and reviewed in dozens of media outlets. In August 2010, O'Dea was recognized with the honor of Champion of Peace, Reconciliation and Forgiveness by the Worldwide Forgiveness Alliance. He was a keynote speaker at the Berlin Peace Festival in August 2011.*

Ascent of the Phoenix:
Global Reconstruction

By Rinaldo Brutoco

WE ARE ON THE VERGE OF WITNESSING THE BIRTH OF A NEW economic order from the ashes of the old. We've been a first-hand witness the last several decades to the dissolution of the old political and economic systems that brought us to this point. And we can now say with some confidence that the time has come for the existing economic order to pass away.

During the past year, the human hunger for social and economic justice has led to an upwelling of protests around the world, from the Arab Spring to the Los Indig-nados movement in Spain to Occupy Wall Street with its many offshoots. These global protests continue to inspire and reenergize each other, creating a new kind of global community.

From an economic view, what has happened that gives rise to this birth of a politicized global conscious-ness? The 2008 financial crisis, the ensuing bank bailouts, the eurozone crisis, and harsh government austerity programs have all starkly revealed the fault lines in the economic systems that protect the rich and the power-ful at the expense of the poor and middle class. So long as the middle class escaped the economic injustices that befell the world's poor, the political will for fundamental change was missing. We're now obviously in another era.

Whether or not the financial system collapses in the near future over the crisis in the eurozone or the unresolved issues left over from the Great Recession, the unacceptable inequities and environmentally destructive practices at the heart of the global economic system show that a systemic change must occur in the way we approach the distribution of goods and services in our global economy.

What we do know is that the distribution of goods and services on the global level is woefully inequitable. We also know that 21,000 children will die today for lack of access to potable water, food, and adequate medical care. Global society has long passed the point economically where half the world's population is enslaved by the global economy. As Abraham Lincoln said before the American Civil War, we cannot long endure "half slave and half free."

The global financial system that was wrapped around this inequitable distribution of goods and services is itself coming apart. We do not yet know whether the final cause of the system's breakup will be the euro crisis, the entry of China as a new dominant player on the field, the disintegration of practical politics in the United States, or other causes as yet unseen. But the destabilizing forces already undermining the existing world order are undeniable.

What we have for a certainty is an economic system in great jeopardy of collapse because it is destroying the planet and leaving far too many people desperate, hungry, thirsty, and uneducated—and far too many children dead—and those tragic statistics are worsening every day. At every level, the economic system isn't working for the vast majority of the seven billion people on the planet.

How do we change the economic system to extend social and economic justice to the vast majority of people? Every person on the planet has a right to adequate potable water, food, medical care, housing, and non-gender-biased education. These are basic human rights.

The greatest act of international charity—the greatest eleemosynary act in human history—occurred in 1947 with the Marshall Plan. The United States decided that if it would help Europe and Japan rebuild their economies, at the very least, the US would be less likely to have another war with Germany and Japan, and they might even become friends.

Germany and Japan not only did not declare another war, but they have gone on to become the United States' closest allies for sixty years. That act of rebuilding a broken Europe and a broken Japan involved the United States spending its money to restore their roads, sewers, schools, highways, manufacturing sectors, and all the things that go into making a civilian society. As the United States spent that money, the country's civilian sector expanded and prospered through meaningful work projects and became the richest society by far in the history of the world.

Out of what was perceived to be an act of charity came the creation of the greatest accumulation of wealth the world has ever known—an explosion of wealth that for fifty years propelled not only the United States but also the entire world forward. The Marshall Plan was a huge success for Europe and Japan, a gargantuan success for the United States, and the single most important component of global prosperity for the entire planet. Talk about "win-win"!

We now stand at the threshold of the next great reconstruction opportunity—and this time it is not limited to Europe and Japan. This time, by enlisting every country in the world in the task, by helping them see that their participation is in their self-interest, a new kind of consciousness will take hold—a consciousness that has evolved to such a point that it chooses to provide everyone on Earth with adequate water, food, shelter, medical care, and education. And that cannot happen by accident.

In fact, with the pressure of climate change upon us, if we do not act quickly, the planet and its inhabitants will be decimated. Those of us who survive will be left trying to reconstruct the planet, but with far fewer resources at our disposal than we currently possess.

We need to look at the opportunity and embrace the fact that we are the people we have been waiting for. The way to have a world that is no longer "half slave and half free" is very simple: free everyone. That's exactly what Lincoln realized during the Civil War and that's what we need to realize today.

The choice is not to economically enslave more people, or to stand by while the number of children dying a day goes from 21,000 to 50,000. The choice is not to stand by casually while the planetary population goes unfed and the biosphere that sustains life is destroyed, causing massive dislocations even of the super-rich in certain countries, along with destitution and poverty everywhere else. The choice is to see that we can solve every single problem in the world—including global population growth, which will fall of its own accord as we raise economic opportunities around the planet. That's precisely the *challenge* and the *opportunity* of global reconstruction.

Global reconstruction is not something we choose to do because we're nice—though it is a nice thing to do. It's not something we choose to do merely because we can't think of anything else to do. We choose to do it because it's the number-one thing that we must do to resolve all our existing problems and dilemmas. It's the only choice a consciously evolved civilization would make.

Having taken on global reconstruction, we will reconstruct the world as we did in 1947 in a way that will add more and more well-being economically, spiritually, and emotionally. And, as we do so, we will see ourselves extending a helping hand to the downtrodden while in the process enriching ourselves.

Like the mythical phoenix bird that rises from the ashes of the dead phoenix consumed by a fire of its own making, a new economy can arise from the death of the old if—as a matter of conscious evolution—we choose to consciously create a system that is radically different from the one that is dying all around us. That new system would be based on the concept of global reconstruction arising out of a profoundly deeper sense of community.

Rinaldo Brutoco is founding president of the World Business Academy, a nonprofit think tank and network founded in 1987 with the mission to educate and inspire business leaders to take responsibility for the planetary whole. Core areas of the Academy's work include sustainable business strategies, the challenge of values-driven leadership, development of the human potential at work, and global reconstruction. In 2007, Rinaldo coauthored his most recent book, Freedom from Mid-East Oil, *a leading book on energy and climate change. A leading executive, writer, and keynote speaker for over twenty-five years, Rinaldo is widely recognized as a practical visionary, change agent, and futurist. He was cofounder and COO of the nation's first pay cable television operation, and CEO of one of the first companies to offer over-the-air TV transmission of major motion pictures. He has served on the board of the Men's Wearhouse, a $2 billion company, for over twenty years, and on numerous nonprofit boards, including the Gorbachev Foundation.*

Our New Story:
Recognizing the Bond

By Lynne McTaggart

JOAN DIDION ONCE OBSERVED THAT WE TELL OURSELVES stories in order to live. Of all our stories, it is the scientific ones that most define us. Those stories create our perception of the universe and how it operates, and from this we shape all our societal structures: our relationships with each other and our environment, our methods of doing business and educating our young, of organizing ourselves into towns and cities, and of defining the borders of our countries and indeed our planet.

Our current scientific story is more than three hundred years old, largely based on the discoveries of Isaac Newton, who described a universe in which all matter was separate and operated according to fixed laws in time and space. The Newtonian vision described a reliable place inhabited by well-behaved and self-contained things. The worldview arising from these discoveries was bolstered by the philosophical implications of Charles Darwin's theory of evolution, with its suggestion that survival is available only to the robustly individual. These, in essence, are stories that idealize a competitive type of separateness. From the moment we are born, we are told that for every winner there must be a loser. From that constricted vision we have fashioned our world.

Although we perceive science as an ultimate truth, science is finally just a story, told in installments. New chapters refine—and often supplant—the chapters that have come before. Because of the scientific discoveries that I have highlighted in my latest three books—*The Field, The Intention Experiment,* and *The Bond*—it is now clear that the story we've been told is about to be replaced by a drastically revised version.

A new understanding is emerging from the laboratories of the most cutting-edge physicists, biologists, and psychologists that challenges the very way we conceive of ourselves. The latest chapter suggests that at our essence, we exist as a unity, a relationship—utterly interdependent, the parts affecting the whole at every moment. Frontier biologists, psychologists, and sociologists have all found evidence that individuals are far less individual than we thought they were. Between the smallest particles of our being, between our body and our environment, between ourselves and all of the people with whom we are in contact, between every member of every societal cluster, there is a *bond*—a connection so integral and profound that there is no longer a clear demarcation between the end of one thing and the beginning of another. The world essentially operates not through the activity of individual things but in the relationship between them—in a sense, *in the space between things.*

These new discoveries in physics and biology demonstrate that all living things succeed and prosper only when they see themselves as part of a greater whole. Rather than a will to compete and dominate, the essential impulse of all of life is a *will to connect.*

The implications of this new story on our understanding of life and the design of our society are extraordinary. They require that we rethink our definitions of ourselves and what exactly it is to be human. If nature has designed us for wholeness, we can no longer think in terms of "winning" and "losing." We need to redefine what we designate as "me" and "not-me." We have to reconsider how we interact with other human beings, choose and carry out our work, structure our communities, and bring up our children. We have to imagine another way to live, an entirely new way to "be." As I wrote in *The Field*, we have to blow up all of our societal creations and begin again, building over scorched ground.

There is a lot of facile thinking about evolution, as if in December 2012 a portal to a new world will simply appear and each of us, stepping through it, will get equipped with a brand new and more evolved consciousness. But making an evolutionary leap—particularly for all of us in the West—is going to require a good deal of conscious, hard work.

Evolving—and by that I mean recovering the life that nature intended us to lead—is going to require a very different set of rules from the ones we currently live by. It is not about fixing what is now broken. It's going to require an ability to envision new ideas for everything, from how we are rewarded for services to each other, to how we relate at every moment. In order to do so, we require nothing less than a major *change of story* about who we are. Most important of all is to reframe the Darwinian idea—deeply embedded in our psyches and in every aspect of our lives—that in order for me to win you have to lose.

Most of us still operate according to the model first proposed by eighteenth-century economist Adam Smith: *We do best for society by looking out for number 1*. This notion underpins our economic system, our educational model, and even our individual and collective relationships.

In order to foster our deep-seated impulses toward cooperation and community, in my book *The Bond* I recommend replacing the Adam Smith model with "the Nash Equilibrium," developed by economist John Nash, which argues that our own best response in any situation is to choose *what is best not only for ourselves but also for the rest of the group.*

Specifically, I suggest that we must evolve in four major areas: we need to perceive the world more holistically, change the very way we relate to people, and organize ourselves differently—in our friendships and neighborhoods, our towns and cities—by enlarging our experience of "community" and learning to come together for common goals.

Finally, we need to change our fundamental purpose on Earth into something more than one based on struggle and domination. Each of us needs to become daily change-agents for generosity and cooperation. As I demonstrate in *The Bond*, a variety of practices focusing on these areas will help people see the world from a more holistic perspective, enjoy more cooperative relationships—even across the deepest divides—develop more united social groups, and become highly infectious spiritual activists in their workplaces and communities.

We have to do nothing less, in other words, than wipe the entire hard drive of our competitive mindset clean. For several centuries we believed in the necessity of survival of the fittest. It has taken a series of crises for us to understand the error in that thinking and to realize that the tool for our rebirth lies in reframing the idea that winning is all about winning over someone else.

© 2012 Lynne McTaggart

Lynne McTaggart is an award-winning journalist and author of six books, including her latest, The Bond *(www.thebond.net), and the worldwide bestsellers* The Intention Experiment *and* The Field, *which have been translated into twenty-eight languages. Lynne is also the architect of the Intention Experiments, the largest mind-over-matter experiments in history (www.theintentionexperiment.com), and cofounder and editorial director of* What Doctors Don't Tell You *(www.wddty. com). McTaggart, her book, and the web-based experiment have been prominently featured in Dan Brown's latest book* The Lost Symbol, *and in the recently released moving documentary,* I Am. *She has been listed as among the world's top one hundred spiritually influential people, and among various accolades, has been referred to as "The Dalai Mama." A member of the Transformational Leadership Council and the Evolutionary Leaders, McTaggart speaks before many diverse audiences around the world. She lives in London with her husband and their two daughters. www.lynnemctaggart.com*

Self-Actualization, Life Purpose, and the Evolutionary Shift

By Jack Canfield

I AM EXCITED ABOUT THE EVOLUTIONARY SHIFT THAT IS occurring at this time in history. I am even more excited to be working with Barbara Marx Hubbard and all the other evolutionary leaders that are helping to facilitate and celebrate this shift in 2012 and beyond. Like many others, my participation in this work is the partial fulfillment of my life purpose, which is to *inspire and empower people to live their highest vision in a context of love and joy in harmony with the highest good of all concerned.*

I first became aware of this purpose more than thirty-five years ago when I was a graduate student in the School of Education at the University of Massachusetts in Amherst. A professor in one of our classes asked us to close our eyes and go back in time to the moment we decided to become a teacher. While some students later reported remembering a teacher who had inspired them and another an experience such as volunteering in a summer school in the south during the civil rights movement, I found myself, quite to my surprise, transported back to before I was born, where I saw myself as a spirit traveling through space with a group of other spirits looking down on Earth during World War II. My awareness of all the chaos, destruction, and suffering that was occurring led me to decide to come down to Earth and be a teacher of peace, love, and joy. At first, the other spirits in the group tried to persuade me not to incarnate. They thought I was being "codependent" and that I should leave well enough alone. However, eventually I convinced most of them to come down with me.

This unexpected and very transformative experience that day convinced me that I was meant to be more than a teacher of social studies (I had previously taught high school for a few years). And that is when I decided to become what I came to call "a teacher with a capital T." From that day on I committed myself to learn everything I could about teaching people to love, value, and respect themselves, each other, and all life on the planet. At first that was manifested in my becoming an expert in the development of self-esteem and self-actualization. Later it evolved into a passion for facilitating self-transcendence, transformational leadership, conscious evolution, social justice, and ecological sustainability.

My experiences have since taught me that social change only occurs when individuals become aware of and learn to trust their own intuitive inner guidance—that is, when they learn to express their own unique gifts and talents, which when fully expressed, ultimately benefit humanity as a whole. I have come to the conclusion after conducting thousands of workshops, trainings, and coaching sessions that everyone is born with a life purpose that they can come to understand and align with, and that when they follow their passions—those things that make them come alive—they are fulfilling that purpose, and perhaps even more importantly, they are fulfilling the evolutionary impulse of all creation being expressed through them.

I have now helped more than a million people all across the globe discover their life purpose and choose to actively align their personal and professional actions with the fulfillment of that purpose. Once they have done this, their lives become more joyful, meaningful, and productive, and they are more able to make a significant contribution to the greater good. I have seen corporate managers become personal development trainers, wealthy housewives open centers for the empowerment of women, lawyers become transformational mediators, traditional doctors become holistic healers, businessmen become major philanthropists, parking attendants become transformational leaders, entrepreneurs become spiritual teachers, politicians become motivational speakers, and even a professor of robotics becomes a leading facilitator of workshops for youth at risk. Most people, once they awaken to their purpose, choose to stay in their chosen professions, but they now approach their work with a deeper set of values, humanity, and compassion.

The human body is made up of trillions of cells, all of which are required to function correctly for the body to operate at full capacity. Similarly, the body of humanity needs every person to fulfill their unique purpose for the world to operate at its highest level of possibility. It is only through each individual fulfilling their unique inborn potential that we will ever create the world we all dream about.

We are at a time in human history when all of us need to step up and have the courage to create the life we envision, that in our heart of hearts we know is possible. We all need to tap into our deepest essence; discover our true life purpose; transcend our fears, limiting beliefs and self-doubts; and live lives of passionate self-expression. When that happens, we will truly create heaven on Earth.

We can already see seeds of this process emerging all over the world. There are numerous schools that encourage students to collaborate rather than compete, to meditate and trust their intuitions, to pursue their unique interests and to passionately follow their dreams. An increasing number of large corporations and small businesses are being consciously managed, socially responsible, and environmentally sustainable. We are witnessing a democratization of the media through the almost universal access to the power of the Internet. Revolutions are occurring in holistic and integrative medicine, a huge growth in organic farming, and an acceleration in the end of ruthless dictatorships around the world. There is much yet to accomplish, but I am optimistic as I see the undeniable evolutionary trends all around the world.

Certainly, just as there is pain to be endured in the birth of a child, there is the pain that accompanies the birth of a new world. As old structures in the economic, political, religious, and educational systems of the world get shaken up, the resulting disruption is definitely painful; but just as in the birth of a child—if one understands and cooperates with rather than resists the process—the pains of labor can be minimized and the miracle of birth can be more deeply and fully experienced.

I believe my role in this process of conscious evolution is to act as a compassionate midwife to our planetary transformation by teaching people to tap into their essential nature, thus allowing it to evolve, expand, and grow in its own self-expression. A first step is to identify and choose to manifest one's unique life purpose. Let me give you one of several processes I use to help you more clearly identify yours. It is a simple technique that you can do right now. All you need is a pen and a piece of paper:

1. First, write down two qualities that you think most accurately describe you. Imagine what your closest friends would say. For me it is *love* and *joy*. For my wife it is *spontaneity* and *authenticity*. For one of my clients who is a professional organizer it is *order* and *harmony*. Write those two qualities on the lines provided below:

_____

_____

2. Next, write down two words that describe how you most like to express those qualities when you are interacting with other people. These should be verbs ending in *–ing*. For me those words are *inspiring* and *teaching*. I inspire people with the more than 20,000 stories I have helped compile and edit in the *Chicken Soup for the Soul* books, which have sold more than 500 million copies around the world. I also empower people with the practical methods, strategies, and techniques I teach people in my Breakthrough to Success seminars, Train the Trainer programs, coaching programs, multimedia programs, and books. Write your two words here:

_____

_____

3. Next, write two or three sentences that describe the world as if it were working perfectly according to you. What would be happening? For me: *Everyone is living their highest vision in harmony with the highest good of all concerned. Everybody is pursuing their dreams in a way that considers their own needs but also is sensitive to the rights and needs of everyone else that is affected by their actions.* Write your description here:

_____

_____

_____

_____

_____

4. Now, combine all three parts into a single description. For example, mine reads: *Inspiring
   and empowering people to live their highest
   vision in a context of love and joy in harmony
   with the highest good of all concerned.* Use the
   space below to write your life purpose statement:

_____

_____

_____

_____

_____

Another way to discover your life purpose is what I call
a "Joy Review." Look back over your life and make a
list of all the times you experienced great joy. One of
my students, Julie Laipley, conducted a Joy Review when
she was preparing to study veterinary medicine while she
was an undergraduate at Ohio State University. She discovered that all her happiest times were when she was

involved in some kind of leadership role or program. She eventually, after some initial resistance, convinced the folks at Ohio State to let her develop an independent study program in leadership and later graduated with OSU's first degree in leadership. After teaching leadership at the Pentagon for a few years, she eventually started her own foundation and now spends her time teaching leadership skills to teenagers and college students throughout the country.

A recent article in Forbes.com listed the top ten happiest jobs as reported by a General Social Survey by the National Organization for Research at the University of Chicago. Not surprisingly, the people that were the happiest were people in jobs where they were following their passion and being of service at the same time. Most of the jobs were not very high paying, but the fulfillment that came from expressing oneself in the service of others seems to provide the greatest level of job satisfaction. Among the ten happiest jobs were clergy, firefighters, physical therapists, authors, special education teachers, teachers, artists, psychologists, and financial service agents. Being a "go-giver" seems to provide more meaningful satisfaction than being a go-getter.

There is a definite trend of more and more people turning inside to find what really fulfills them. As each of us has the courage to step fully into that which lights us up, we will see a world in which enlightened behavior is the norm rather than the exception. I believe that world is right around the corner.

Jack Canfield is the CEO of the Canfield Training Group in Santa Barbara, California. He is the cocreator of the New York Times *bestselling* Chicken Soup for the Soul® *series, which has 215 titles and has sold more than 500 million books in forty-seven languages around the world. He is also the coauthor of the* The Success Principles, Heart at Work, The Key to Living the Law of Attraction, *and* The Golden Motorcycle Gang. *He is the founder of the Transformational Leadership Council and a member of Evolutionary Leaders. He has appeared in the mov-ies* The Secret, The Meta-Secret, The Truth, Discover the Gift, Tapping the Source, *and* The Keeper of the Keys. *His website is www.JackCanfield.com.*

Part 4

RESOURCES FOR
THE BIRTH

RECOMMENDED RESOURCES

Foundation for Conscious Evolution

www.evolve.org

The Foundation for Conscious Evolution is a nonprofit educational institution cofounded in 1990 by Barbara Marx Hubbard and Sidney Lanier. Its mission is to educate, communicate, and activate humanity's potential for self and social evolution. Its ultimate goal is an awakened humanity in harmony with nature—for the highest good of all life.

The Foundation's initiatives offer a context and a container for connecting and empowering the global movements for positive change, making the efforts of this movement visible to engender greater coherence and synergy. Its website contains a comprehensive list of the works of Barbara Marx Hubbard along with initiatives, programs, and evolutionary educational offerings.

evolve

Forming Evolutionary Communities

A Special Project of the Foundation for Conscious Evolution

www.evolve.org

By forming evolutionary communities, people can deepen their experience of self and social evolution and create sustainable communities of shared purpose, cocreation, and service to society during the Great Shift. My friend and thought partner, Judy Cauley, CSJ, and Patricia Gaul, executive director of the Foundation for Conscious Evolution, are working with me to develop new tools and teachings to support these goals. We are committed to providing people with a developmental path to foster conscious evolution in their daily lives. Because the need to evolve consciously and collectively is now an evolutionary imperative, our foundation is offering Stepping Into the Field of Conscious Evolution. This program contributes to the formation of a developmental path in our human evolution and is based on my work. It contains ideas, tools, resources and capacities—a new memetic code—that anyone would need to know to practice self and social evolution toward the planetary shift.

Stepping Into the Field of Conscious Evolution provides a three-step evolutionary arc that is designed for personal use or for the growth of evolutionary communities, consisting of three elements: "Awakening to Conscious Evolution," "Deepening in Conscious Evolution," and "Living Conscious Evolution." Each of these three interrelated components can be taken separately or as a self-paced sequence of all three.

We envision people in Circles and Hub communities everywhere building the field of conscious evolution and shaping a cocreative society, and we see this work as the greatest experience they can have of evolutionary education. The most significant act of our time is the formation of evolutionary communities.

—Barbara Marx Hubbard

The Shift from Ego to Essence

*Join the global community of self-evolving
pioneers in the Emergence Process*

www.evolve.org

The Emergence Process is for those of us who are awakening now to something new within ourselves and are yearning to give our gifts to heal and transform our world. It is a spiritual path designed exactly for this moment in history when we are facing societal breakdowns and breakthroughs on an unprecedented scale. Our very survival and that of other species depend upon us making the shift individually and collectively from ego-driven behavior to a more spiritual way of being and acting.

I have joined with my familial sister, Patricia Ellsberg—a social change activist, meditation teacher, and evolutionary coach—to offer the Emergence Process. In this work, we shift our identity from ego to essence; we give birth to ourselves as Universal Humans, connected through the heart to the whole of life, expanding into cosmic consciousness. We learn to *become* our Essential Self, experiencing the joy of the union of the human and divine within.

This practice is an evolutionary requirement for us to bring our full potential self into the world. Otherwise we remain limited by the sufferings of our separated ego. Shifting in this way is essential for our personal fulfillment and our ability to contribute our greatest gifts to the Planetary Shift—in time to gentle the Birth.

—Barbara Marx Hubbard

I am in love with the Emergence Process. It enables us to transcend our separated egoic self, which often is anxious and fearful, and learn to live as our Essential Self—wise, loving, powerful, and radiant. It helps us heal the wounded parts of our ego, or sub-personalities, by lifting them up into the vibrational field of our essence so that we can live at a higher frequency.

Inspired by the story of Barbara's own emergence, the Emergence Process takes us on a joyful journey of self-discovery. Guided by practices, deep meditations, and questions for reflection and journal writing, we learn to walk this mystical path with practical feet. We are able to repattern our lives so that we live with more ease, confidence, creativity, and purpose. We embody more fully the qualities that our hearts desire: wisdom, love, joy, and peace. We become the Beloved we are seeking.

As Einstein said, "You cannot solve a problem on the same level of consciousness that created it. You must learn to see the world anew." Never before has it been more important that we elevate our consciousness and evolve ourselves so we can help evolve our world.

—Patricia Ellsberg

For more about the Emergence Process and the revised edition of Barbara's book, *Emergence: The Shift from Ego to Essence,* please see: www.evolve.org.

The Birth 2012 Campaign

Cocreating the Planetary Shift

www.Birth2012.com

Are you being called to help create a healthy, prosperous, peaceful, and sustainable world? Are you preparing to give your Gift to the Shift? Do you want to help generate a "tipping point" that will accelerate the Birth? Barbara Marx Hubbard is partnering with The Shift Network, the Welcoming Committee, and thousands like you in a global initiative to "gentle the Birth" and transform all sectors of global society. Barbara's Birth 2012 Campaign will symbolically inaugurate this new era on December 22, 2012 as part of a massive global celebration of the Planetary Birth Day. Join millions around the world committed to ushering in this great transition by using Birth2012.com as your hub of activity. This multi-featured site provides:

- **Book Information:** Discover all things having to do with Birth 2012 and Beyond, including eBook versions, QR-code videos, book reviews, and news about Barbara's extensive campaign and book tour.

- **Campaign News:** Read articles, blogs, and updates about all aspects of the worldwide Birth 2012 effort at "Campaign Central."

- **Tools for Organizing:** Find tools for working collaboratively within the Wheel of Cocreation across all sectors and scales, including: engaging in "Hub activities"; creating Shift Circles, Town Hall Meetings in the Round, or Syncons; or jump-starting your own collaborative efforts.

- **Vocational Support:** Discover your vocation of destiny and match your resources, skills, and ideas with real needs—locally and globally; connect with thousands of innovators online through links to ShiftMovement.com.

- **Events:** Track with all Birth 2012-related events; find out what is happening when and where, and plug into those events that resonate with your passions.

- **Access to Sponsors and Allies:** Link to Birth 2012 Campaign sponsors and collaborators, including Welcoming Committee members and their organizations.

**Make Birth2012.com your
Birth 2012 Campaign headquarters!**

The Vistar Foundation
Building Evolutionary Shift Circles

www.vistarfoundation.org

The Vistar Method evolved over sixteen years of committed, cutting-edge work on convening Circles. Its format is uniquely suited for collective evolutionary awakening in support of the Birth.

The Method follows four guidelines and a simple structure. The guidelines, called GuideRules, are deeply rooted in metaphysical principles that are easy to apply. The Vistar GuideRules address the focusing of attention and energy in a group so that the whole can move to new levels of understanding, connection, and meaning. The Method's disciplined format allows transformative meetings where individuals can break through barriers to authenticity and work together synergistically. The creators of Vistar, Ron Friedman, MD, and Victoria Friedman, also point to a less tangible factor, "the magic of conscious partnership with the Creative Source, which can uplift and infuse gatherings with a sense of unity and meaning and a vision of purpose. It's about energy, clarity, and moving beyond the quagmires and barriers experienced in normal group communication in evolutionary groups, businesses, in families, and certainly on the world stage."

The Vistar Method is easy to learn and can be used for a small or large number of participants. It defines three roles for each meeting: the Leader, the Support, and the Participant, each with their own responsibility to the Circle.

I have found that, as the frequency of a meeting increases, the direct heartfelt experience of connectedness emerges and, with it, immense new possibilities. The

Vistar Method is an art form, a cocreative social structure, and a promising approach for starting a Shift Circle.

—Barbara Marx Hubbard

The Cocreative Society

Creators of the Virtual Syncon

www.co-creative-society.com

The Cocreative Society has been formed by a remarkable and dedicated group of students of Barbara Marx Hubbard. This group's goal is to discover what a cocreative society is like. In their work they have found, among other things, that the key to cocreation is resonance, the echoing back of the highest in each other. They have produced a book on that subject: the 144-page *Virtual Syncon Manual*. They have also developed a remarkable process called a Virtual Syncon, which is now being tested. Its purpose is to bring people together in every sector of the Wheel of Cocreation to find their vocations, nurture their projects, discover partners, and actually fulfill their goals through matching needs and resources. They see the current Virtual Syncon process becoming a global online Syncon available worldwide. The Cocreative Society now offers open participation for all in its annual Virtual Syncon events. It also provides consulting for conducting a Syncon in your community—virtually or "on the ground"—and are also prepared to assist with Town Hall Meetings in the Round, Syncon style.

RECOMMENDED READING

Books by Barbara Marx Hubbard

— *The Evolutionary Journey: A Personal Guide to a Positive Future.* Evolutionary Press, 1982.

— *The Hunger of Eve: One Woman's Odyssey Toward the Future.* Island Pacific Northwest, 1989.

— *The Revelation: A Message of Hope for the New Millennium.* Nataraj Publishing, 1995.

— *The Evolutionary Communion: The Sacred Way of Conscious Evolution* (guidebook with CD). Foundation for Conscious Evolution, 2011.

— *52 Codes for Conscious Self Evolution: A Process of Metamorphosis to Realize Our Full Potential Self.* Foundation for Conscious Evolution, 2011.

— *Emergence: The Shift from Ego to Essence.* Hampton Roads, 2001.

— *Conscious Evolution: Awakening the Power of Our Social Potential.* New World Library, 1998 (new edition forthcoming in 2012).

Works Recommended by Barbara

Abrams, Nancy Ellen, and Joel R. Primack. *The New Universe and the Human Future: How a Shared Cosmology Could Transform the World.* Yale University Press, 2011.

Anderson, Carolyn, with Katharine Roske. *The Co-Creators Handbook: An Experiential Guide for Discovering Your Life's Purpose and Building a Co-creative Society.* Global Family, 2001.

Aurobindo, Sri. *The Life Divine.* Lotus Press/Sri Aurobindo Centenary Library, 1972.

Bache, Christopher M. *Dark Night, Early Dawn: Steps to a Deep Ecology of Mind.* State University of New York Press, 2000.

Berry, Thomas. *The Great Work: Our Way into the Future.* Bell Tower, 1999.

Berry, Thomas. *The Dream of the Earth.* Sierra Club Books, 1988.

Bruteau, Beatrice. *God's Ecstasy: The Creation of a Self-Creating World.* Crossroad Publishing, 1997.
— *The Grand Option: Personal Transformation and a New Creation.* University of Notre Dame Press, 2001.

Canfield, Jack, and William Gladstone. *The Golden Motorcycle Gang: A Story of Transformation,* Hay House, 2011.

Cannato, Judy. *Radical Amazement: Contemplative Lessons from Black Holes, Supernovas, and Other Wonders of the Universe.* Sorin Books, 2006.

Chaisson, Eric. *The Life Era: Cosmic Selection and Conscious Evolution.* W.W. Norton, 1989; iUniverse, 2000.

Teilhard de Chardin, Pierre. *The Phenomenon of Man. Harper Perennial Modern Classics,* 2008.
— *The Human Phenomenon,* Sussex Academic Press, 1999.
— *The Divine Milieu, Perennial Classics,* Harper & Row, 1960.

Delio, Ilia. *The Emergent Christ.* Orbis Books, 2011.

Dowd, Michael. *Thank God for Evolution: How the Marriage of Science and Religion Will Transform Your Life and Our World.* Plume, 2009.

Elgin, Duane. *The Living Universe: Where Are We? Who Are We? Where Are We Going?* Berrett-Koehler Publishers, 2009.

Gardner, James N. *Biocosm: The New Scientific Theory of Evolution.* Inner Ocean, 2003.

Haught, John F. *Making Sense of Evolution: Darwin, God, and the Drama of Life.* Westminster John Knox Press, 2010.

Hawken, Paul. *Blessed Unrest: How the Largest Social Movement in History Is Restoring Grace, Justice, and Beauty to the World*. The Penguin Group, 2008.

Kurzweil, Ray. *The Singularity is Near: When Humans Transcend Biology*. Viking, 2005.

Lanier, Sydney. *The Sovereign Person: A Soul's Call to Conscious Evolution*. Foundation for Conscious Evolution, 2010.

Laszlo, Ervin. *The Chaos Point: 2012 and Beyond: Appointment with Destiny*. Hampton Roads Publishing, 2010.
— *Science and the Akashic Field: An Integral Theory of Everything*. Inner Traditions, 2007.

LeCain, Eleanor. *Breakthrough Solutions: How to Improve Your Life and Change the World by Building What Works*. New Way Press, 2012.

Lipton, Bruce. *The Biology of Belief: Unleashing the Power of Consciousness, Matter, & Miracles*, Hay House, 2007.

McTaggert, Lynne. *The Bond: Connecting Through the Space Between Us*. Free Press, 2011.

Pearce, Joseph Chilton. *The Crack in the Cosmic Egg: New Constructs of Mind and Reality*. Park Street Press, 2002.

Russell, Peter. *Waking Up in Time: Finding Inner Peace in Times of Accelerating Change*. Origin Press, 2008.

Swimme, Brian Thomas and Mary Evelyn Tucker, *Journey of the Universe.* Yale University Press, 2011.

Swimme, Brian and Thomas Berry. *The Universe Story: From the Primordial Flaring Forth to the Ecozoic Era.* Harper San Francisco, 1992.

Lynne Twist, *The Soul of Money: Reclaiming the Wealth of Our Inner Resources.* W.W. Norton, 2003.

Walsch, Neale Donald. *The Mother of Invention: The Legacy of Barbara Marx Hubbard and the Future of YOU.* Hay House, 2011.

AFFILIATED ORGANIZATIONS

Birth 2012 Campaign Sponsors

Our sponsors are like-minded organizations that fully support the Birth 2012 Campaign and have helped to build our momentum through sharing this movement with their networks. We highly recommend collaborating with these groups who share our goal of cocreating a collective shift. To explore Birth 2012 sponsorship for your organization, please contact marykay@theshiftnetwork.com.

Common Passion is a global social collaborative of individuals and communities who share compassion as a common passion. They orchestrate global meditations and prayer events with all faith and wisdom traditions with an intention of creating harmony through science-based and faith-based applications of collective consciousness. www.commonpassion.org

CSRwire is a source of corporate social responsibility and sustainability news, reports, events, and information. www.csrwire.com

Daily Om is dedicated to nurturing mind, body, and spirit. www.dailyom.com

Dream University creates practical and motivational programs that turn dreams into life's reality. www.dreamuniversity.com

Excellerated Business Schools® helps students unleash their entrepreneurial spirit and power.
www.excellerated.com

Finer Minds is a collection of inspiring personal growth stories and videos.
www.finerminds.com

The Gaiafield Project develops subtle activism principles, theories, practices, and programs, to cocreate a global network of subtle activists for social and planetary transformation.
www.gaiafield.net

The Gandhi King Seasons for Peace and Nonviolence (SPAN) offers a new model for spiritually-based grassroots citizen leadership, igniting a fusion of new communities and initiatives. SPAN celebrates four "seasons" each year during which almost any theme and action can be harbored, and provides you as a leader with free tools and resources that help you grow your vision.
www.spiritualactivism.net

The Global Coherence Initiative is a science-based, co-creative project to unite people in heart-focused care and intention, to facilitate a shift in global consciousness.
www.glcoherence.org

Good Life Networks is a transformational content aggregator that provides the modular functionality needed for teachers, thought leaders, and guides to distribute their messages throughout the world via radio, television, Internet, publishing, and all forms of digital media, including mobile and tablets.
www.GoodLifeNetworks.com

Green America is a nonprofit membership organization (founded in 1982 originally under the name "Co-op America") to harness the strength of consumers, investors, businesses, and the marketplace to create a socially just and environmentally sustainable society.
www.greenamerica.org

Humanity's Team is a spiritual movement whose purpose is to communicate and implement a belief that we are all one with God and life, so that the behavior of humanity may shift to reflect this understanding.
www.humanitysteam.org

Institute of HeartMath is a research and educational organization dedicated to creating tools that allow individuals to reduce stress, self-regulate emotions, and increase energy and resilience in order to live healthier, more productive, and happier lives. The vision and quest for global heart coherence is the primary mission of HeartMath.
www.heartmath.org

Intent is a website and community that connects you with others to announce and receive support for your day-to-day intentions.
www.intent.com

The Heart of the Healer Foundation is a catalyst for the emergence of a planetary family living in sacred relationship with Earth Mother by bridging the gap between indigenous cultural traditions and the modern world.
www.heartofthehealer.org

The Hendricks Institute teaches core skills for conscious living and conscious loving. Over the past three decades they have assisted people in opening to more creativity, love, and vitality through the power of conscious

relationship and whole-person learning.
www.hendricks.com

Maestro Conference is a powerful online collaborative teleconferencing platform.
www.maestroconference.com

Mindvalley publishes personal growth products designed to help you awaken the hidden power of your mind, body and spirit.
www.mindvalley.com

National Peace Academy nurtures cultures of peace by conducting research and facilitating learning toward the development of peace systems and the development of the full spectrum of the peacebuilder.
www.nationalpeaceacademy.us

ONE Becoming ONE began with connecting the individuals, communities, and organizations that exemplify a world whose foundational principles are love, collaboration, and social healing, as well as watching those principles in action spread through all sectors of business, society, and civic engagement.
www.onetheevent.org

Peace 2012 is uniting all humanity in a shared experience of peaceful gathering in which we all stop and reflect on what we have in common, rather than what divides us.
www.peace2012.net

The Peace Alliance empowers civic engagement toward a culture of peace through an alliance of organizers and advocates throughout the United States taking the work of peacebuilding from the margins of society into the centers of national discourse and policy-making.
www.thepeacealliance.org

Sacred Centers, founded by Anodea Judith, PhD, is a teaching organization that uses the map of the chakra system for an embodied awakening of individual awareness and the evolution of global consciousness.
www.sacredcenters.com

Wake Up Laughing is led by Swami Beyondananda, who is the cosmic comic alter ego of writer, humorist, performer, and uncommontator Steve Bhaerman. The Swami, whose favorite yoga pose is tongue-in-cheek, is the spokesperson for a new non-religion, FUNdamentalism (accent on the "fun"). Says the Swami, "We are strictly non-dominational."
www.wakeuplaughing.com

World Business Academy is a business think tank and network of business and thought leaders founded in 1986 with the mission of inspiring and helping business assume responsibility for the whole of society.
www.worldbusiness.org

WorldPeace.org spreads the universal peace message and prayer "May Peace Prevail On Earth" far and wide to embrace the lands and people of this Earth.
www.worldpeace.org

Worldshift Media is a social-enterprise coalition that promotes the values of peace, justice, sustainability, social innovation, and conscious evolution.
www.worldshiftmedia.org

11:11 Magazine provides soulfully satisfying bi-monthly journalism for the seeker on the journey.
www.1111mag.com

Shift Network Allies

These diverse organizations and individuals offer complementary work that advances personal, social, and collective evolution. We heartily recommend them all.

Bioneers brings together social and scientific innovators from all disciplines to study, discuss, and disseminate solutions to major environmental and social issues. Thousands attend the annual Bioneers Conference, connecting through a network of networks, with hundreds of thousands of people dedicated to creating positive change for a sustainable world.
www.bioneers.org

Club of Budapest is a global organization that was founded in 1993 by systems theorist and philosopher Dr. Ervin Laszlo. The mission for the Club of Budapest is to serve as a catalyst for the transformation to a sustainable world through the promotion of the emergence of a planetary consciousness. The club has a unique focus on integrating spirituality, science, and the arts and interconnecting generations and cultures.
www.clubofbudapest.org, www.worldshift2012.org
www.worldshiftmovement.org

Esalen Institute is located in the heart of Big Sur, California, and has provided pioneering workshops to more than 300,000 people over the last five decades. Esalen has focused on events and trainings that encourage exploring new possibilities and creating states of higher awareness.
www.esalen.org

Four Years. Go. is a communication and commitment campaign to create the collective will that is needed to shift the course of history so that, by the end of 2014, humanity is on the pathway to a thriving, just, sustainable future for all. www.fouryearsgo.org

Institute of Noetic Sciences was founded in 1973 by Apollo 14 astronaut Edgar Mitchell with the mission to support individual and collective transformation through consciousness research and educational outreach. "Noetic" comes from the Greek word *nous*, which means "intuitive mind" or "inner knowing." www.noetic.org

Omega Institute for Holistic Studies, founded in 1977, is a center for wellness and personal growth. Located on 195 acres in Rhinebeck, New York, in the Hudson Valley—as well as other locations around the world. Omega welcomes tens of thousands of people to its workshops, conferences, and retreats. Omega's mission is to provide innovative educational experiences that awaken the best in the human spirit, providing hope and healing for individuals and society. www.eomega.org

Pachamama Alliance provides legal services and makes available training and consulting on indigenous people's collective and legal rights under local, national, and international law. www.pachamama.org

Unify Earth is a global spectacle planned for December 21, 2012. Its goal is to present a performance entitled "Urth," featuring Cirque du Soleil and other major artists, at the Mayan site of Chichen Itza in Mexico, to be broadcast worldwide. This event will culminate in a moment of global unity. In the months leading up to the

event, Unify Earth will create a global resource network and viral media campaign that will provide practical tools and techniques for humanity to bring about a positive transformation of our planetary culture.
www.unifyearth.com

Evolutionary Leaders
www.evolutionaryleaders.net

Evolutionary Leaders is an association that provides opportunities for synergistic engagement among leaders committed to the conscious evolution of humanity. Its members are important individual allies of our campaign for the Birth, and many are direct supporters and frequent collaborators with Barbara Marx Hubbard. The members of EL include the following:

Don Beck—www.spiraldynamics.net
Michael Beckwith—www.agapelive.com
Joan Borysenko—www.joanborysenko.com
Gregg Braden—www.greggbraden.com
Patrick Brauckmann—
    www.evolutionaryleaders.net/leaders/pbrauckmann
Rinaldo Brutoco—www.worldbusiness.org
Jack Canfield—www.jackcanfield.com
Scott Carlin—gatecommunity.org
Deepak Chopra —www.chopra.com
Andrew Cohen—www.andrewcohen.org
Oran Cohen—www.evolutionaryleaders.net/
    leaders/ocohen
Dale Colton—www.sourceofsynergyfoundation.org
Wendy Craig-Purcell—www.wendycraigpurcell.com
Stephen Dinan—www.theshiftnetwork.com
Michael Dowd—www.evolutionarytimes.org
Gordon Dveirin—
    www.evolutionaryleaders.net/leaders/gdveirin
Duane Elgin—www.awakeningearth.org
Barbara Fields—www.agnt.org

Ashok Gangadean—awakeningmind.org
Kathleen Gardarian—www.qualisintl.com
Tom Gegax—
    www.evolutionaryleaders.net/leaders/tgegax
David Gershon—www.empowermentinstitute.net
Mark Gerzon—www.markgerzon.com
Charles Gibbs—www.uri.org
Joshua Gorman—www.generationwakingup.org
Craig Hamilton—www.integralenlightenment.com
Kathy Hearn—www.revkathy.com
Jean Houston—www.jeanhouston.com
Ervin Laszlo—www.clubofbudapest.org
Bruce Lipton—www.brucelipton.com
Lynnaea Lumbard—www.newstories.org
Elza S. Maalouf—www.globalfeminine.org
Howard Martin—www.heartmath.com
Fred Matser—www.startfundglobal.org
Rod McGrew—www.sourceofsynergyfoundation.org
Steve McIntosh—www.stevemcintosh.com
Lynne McTaggart—www.theintentionexperiment.com
Nipun Mehta—www.nipun.charityfocus.org
Nina Meyerhof—www.children-of-the-earth.org
Deborah Moldow—www.worldpeace.org
James O'Dea—www.jamesodea.com
Terry Patten—www.gobeyondawakening.com
Carter Phipps—www.enlightennext.org
Ocean Robbins—www.oceanrobbins.com
Peter Russell—www.peterrussell.com
Elisabet Sahtouris—www.sahtouris.com
Yuka Saionji—www.goipeace.or.jp
Gerard Senehi—www.gerardsenehi.com
Christian Sorensen—www.seasidecenter.com
Emily Squires—
    www.evolutionaryleaders.net/leaders/esquires
Daniel Stone—www.danielstone.com
Lynne Twist—
    www.fouryearsgo.org, www.pachamama.org

Diane Williams—www.sourceofsynergyfoundation.org
Katherine Woodward Thomas—
    www.katherinewoodwardthomas.com
Tom Zender—www.tomzender.com

Transformational Leadership Council

Members of the Transformational Leadership Council (TLC) are also individual allies of our work. It includes CEOs, trainers, facilitators, thought leaders, authors, movie producers and directors, and coaches—all of whom are focused on transformational leadership. Many are closely collaborating with the Birth 2012 Campaign. TLC's members include the following:

Raymond Aaron—www.monthlymentor.com
Arjuna Ardagh—www.awakeningcoachingtraining.com
Alison Armstrong—www.understandmen.com
William Arntz—www.whatthebleep.com/makers/#will
Chris Attwood—www.enlightenedalliances.com
Janet Attwood—www.thepassiontest.com
Patty Aubery—www.chickensoupforthesoul.com
Barnet Bain—www.barnetbain.com
Anat Baniel—www.anatbanielmethod.com
Blaine Bartlett—www.avatar-resources.com
Bill Bauman—www.billbauman.net
Michael Bernard Beckwith—www.agapelive.com
Rickie Byars Beckwith—www.agapelive.com
Pete Bissonette—www.learningstrategies.com
Ray Blanchard—www.rayblanchard.com
Nicole Brandon—www.nicolebrandonworldwide.com
Lee Brower—www.quadrantliving.com
David Buck—www.coachville.com
Jim Bunch—www.jimbunch.com
Inga Canfield—www.chickensoupforthesoul.com

Jack Canfield—www.jackcanfield.com
Sonia Choquette—www.soniachoquette.com
John Chupka—www.forgivenesscenter.org
Joyce Quaranta Chupka—
    www.joycequarantachupka.com
Cherie Clark—www.doinglife.com
Scott Coady—www.embodiedwisdom.com
Chip Conley—www.emotionalequations.com
DC Cordova—www.excellerated.com
Patricia Coughlin—www.patriciacoughlin.com
Stephen Covey—www.coveylink.com
Sydney Cresci—www.makeachangejourneys.com
Steve D'Annunzio—www.theprosperityparadigm.com
Gordon Davidson—www.joyfulevolution.net
Zen DeBrücke—www.smartsoulacademy.com
John Carpenter Dealey—www.smileworld.com
John Demartini—www.drdemartini.com
Scott deMoulin—www.destinytraining.com
Bobbi DePorter—www.qln.com
Marie Diamond—www.mariediamond.com
Mike Dooley—www.tut.com
Ken Druck—www.jennadruckcenter.org
Joanne Dunleavy—www.newagreementscoaching.com
Hale Dwoskin—www.sedona.com
Eric Edmeades—www.ericedmeades.com
Peter Einstein—www.ecoactiveamerica.com
Dave Ellis—www.fallingawake.com
Joan Emery—www.belvedereconsultants.com
Stewart Emery—www.belvedereconsultants.com
Roxanne Emmerich—www.roxanneemmerich.com
Cheryl Esposito—www.alexsaconsulting.com
Rob Evans—www.collaborationengine.ca/team
Arielle Ford—www.arielleford.com
Mike Foster—www.fosterinstitute.com
Bill Galt—
    futureshapers.ning.com/profile/williamandrewgalt
Lisa Garr—www.theawareshow.com

John Gray—www.marsvenus.com
Deirdre Hade—www.deirdrehade.com
Jim Hardt—www.biocybernaut.com
Roger James Hamilton—www.rogerjameshamilton.com
Gay Hendricks—www.hendricks.com
Christine Hibbard—www.christinehibbard.org
Raz Ingrasci—www.hoffmaninstitute.org
Lise Janelle—www.centreforheartliving.com
Fred Johnson—www.frejon.org
Stephen Josephs—www.leadershipagility.com
Cynthia Kersey—www.unstoppable.net
Jim Kwik—www.jimkwik.com
Morty Lefkoe—www.lefkoeinstitute.com
Shelly Lefkoe—www.speakingwithoutfear.com
Chunyi Lin—www.springforestqigong.com
Willson Lin—www.doers.cn
Greg Link—www.coveylink.com
Robert MacPhee—www.heartset.com
Jeddah Mali—www.jeddahmali.com
Fabrizio Mancini—www.parkercc.edu
Alex Mandossian—www.alexmandossian.com
Howard Martin—www.heartmath.com
Marcia Martin—www.1degreetv.com
Scott Martineau—www.consciousone.com
Tom McCarthy—www.tommccarthy.com
Peggy McColl—www.destinies.com
Mark McKergow—www.sfwork.com
Corinne McLaughlin—www.visionarylead.org
Lynne McTaggart—www.wddty.com
EnRico Melson—www.globalintegrativemedicine.net
Ivan Misner—www.bni.com
Dianne Morrison—www.morrisonmcnabb.com
Mary Morrissey—www.www.marymorrissey.com
Sue Morter—www.drsuemorter.com
Lisa Nichols—www.lisa-nichols.com
Gabriel Nossovitch—www.gabrieln.com
Nick Ortner—www.thetappingsolution.com

Steve Pavlina—www.stevepavlina.com
John Perkins—www.johnperkins.org
James Redmond—www.dynamicvideos.net
Neal Rogin—www.awakeninguniverse.com
Genpo Roshi—www.genpo.org
Deborah Rozman—www.quantumintech.com
Martin Rutte—www.martinrutte.com
Paul Scheele—www.learningstrategies.com
Nancy Salzman—www.nxivm.com
Robert Scheinfeld—www.bobscheinfeld.com
Jim Selman—www.paracomm.com
Marci Shimoff—www.marcishimoff.com
Yakov Smirnoff—www.yakov.com
Jana Stanfield—www.janastanfield.com
Donna Steinhorn—www.coachingtosuccess.com
Guy Stickney—www.conversationamongmasters.com
Orjan Strindlund—www.coachpower.se
Terry Tillman—www.227company.com
Lynne Twist—www.soulofmoney.org
Nina Rothschild Utne—
     www.bioneers.org/presenters/nina-rothschild-utne
Joe Vitale—www.joevitale.com
Matt Weinstein—www.playfair.com
Maggie Weiss—www.pacificedge.us
Marcia Wieder—www.dreamuniversity.com
Marianne Williamson—www.marianne.com
Jane (JC) Willhite—www.psiseminars.com
Mikki Willis—www.elevatecollective.com
Stephanie Wolf—www.sportsmind.com
David TS Wood—www.davidtraining.com
Sandra Yancey—www.ewomennetwork.com
Tyson Young

SPECIAL ESSAYS

Evolutionary Creativity: What Is It, Who Does It, Why Does It Matter?

By Jan Phillips

PEOPLE OFTEN DENY THEIR CREATIVE POTENTIAL. THEY say things like "I'm not creative. I can't even draw a straight line." Or "I'm not artistic. I can't paint." There is an assumption that being creative has something to do with painting or drawing straight lines. Claiming to be creative feels like an arrogant thing to say about yourself if you're not an expert, not making a living from your creations, not well-known and publicly acclaimed for your imaginative gifts. But creativity is much bigger than that.

Creativity is the gift we *all* have that enables us to convert our experiences into other forms—into stories, poems, songs, gardens, recipes, quilts. Every day we encounter a myriad of people and adventures. We talk with people. We work with people. We argue and laugh and plan with people. Then we create stories about our interactions. Every day we wake up with a blank canvas of twenty-four hours. We call it our "day"—but it's really our canvas for creating our life.

Day by day, choice by choice, thought by thought, word by word, we create our lives. And as our intentions and energies seep out beyond the boundaries of our flesh and intermingle with the intentions and energies of others, we engage in the cocreation of our families, our communities, our cultures, and ultimately, our civilization. If you're breathing, you're creating something—even if it's nothing more than the energy field a person walks into when they are near you.

We know from science that our electromagnetic field (em field) extends from eight to twelve feet beyond our bodies. As noted elsewhere in this book, the Institute of HeartMath performed several studies to investigate the possibility that the em field generated by the heart may transmit information that can be received by others. They concluded that the heart's em field is an important carrier of information, so when two people are at a conversational distance, the electromagnetic signal generated by one person's heart can influence the other person's brain rhythms. For the first time, there is scientific proof that a compassionate heart can actually bring peace to the room.

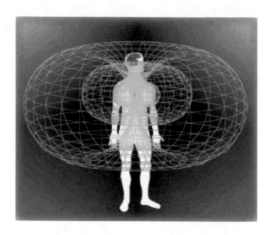

If in your heart you have generated peace, compassion, loving kindness, then that's exactly what others experience when they are in your presence. You create in the world what you hold in your heart.

Years ago, we didn't have the equipment to measure this kind of phenomenon. We never understood that we literally, consciously *create* the entire em field around ourselves—that we create how it *feels* for others to be around us. We tend to hold creativity in a small box that was related to paints, colors, the arts, ballet, opera, Russian novels. Most of us have been taught not to think of ourselves as "creative." If a child went to a parent saying s/he wanted to be an artist when s/he grew up, the parent might say, " Oh honey, you can't make any money as an artist. You'll have to be something else." And that child's creativity would rarely thrive. Their imagination would not be nurtured.

We know that our imagination is the most potent engine of change in the world. In the past year, we have watched people's commitment and creativity topple oppressive regimes, stop wars, challenge the status quo, and connect people around the globe. Our creativity is the *manifestation* of our consciousness. It is our thoughts, our prayers, our words made flesh. And what makes our creativity *evolutionary* is the additional factor of our *regard for the common good.*

If I am conscious of how I use my energy, manage my thoughts, compose my words, create my days, then I am a conscious creator, an evolutionary creator. I am aware that I am engaged in evolution as an *agent*. It is not happening *to* me. It is happening *through* me. The world is in the throes of an evolutionary shift and evolutionary creators are consciously contributing to it, weighing in on the side of fairness, compassion, justice. A conscious-evolution movement is afoot and those who are in it know that. They are proud of it, committed to it, filled with hope and humbled by the great mystery and wonder of it all.

Psychologist Mihaly Csikszentmihalyi, author of *Creativity: Flow and the Psychology of Discovery and Invention* says that creativity doesn't happen in our heads but in the interaction between our imagination and our social context. It's a matter of experience and response, a matter of *relationship to others* and a commentary on the significance of our encounters. Creativity is the vivid expression of who we are in the cosmos.

The world is not divided into two groups, the creative people and the not-creative people. If there's a distinction, it's between those who are creatively productive and those with unexpressed potential. We're all creative by default. We're genetically predisposed to create. Each of us, to varying degrees, is intrinsically motivated to be original and to solve challenging problems. The question to ask is not, "Am I creative?" but rather, "What inspires me and how can I share that?"

Creativity is not about intelligence or information. It's about inspiration, from the Latin *spiritus,* meaning "breath, courage, the soul." Creativity is about being fully alive, living courageously, or as the painter Joan Miro´ says, "Expressing with precision all the gold sparks the soul gives off." We inspire each other when we dare to create. We open others' hearts. We unlock their doors so their spirits can soar. And this is *why* it matters: the path through the dark forest can be lit by our work. Others can find their courage in the creations we conjure. Our stories can help people see these times in a new way, understand that this chaos is only a local view of the cosmos evolving beautifully.

When we join in as conscious cocreators, we are fulfilling our nature, midwifing the new even as we are *made* anew. We are looking at the tipping point our planet is facing and nudging it toward life. We are saying YES to the future, YES to our grandchildren, YES to the creatures that share this land. And that affirmation of life is what brings us life, that we may have it more abundantly. Dualities are giving way to the singular. Polarities are dissolving into unity. Earth is giving birth to a species that celebrates its oneness with All That Is. Yes, we are evolving, and the light is on its way!

Jan Phillips is an artist/activist and the author of several books. She leads workshops throughout the year in evolutionary creativity and spiritual consciousness. Jan is also executive director and cofounder of the Livingkindness Foundation, an international collaboration of grassroots philanthropists. Jan's interview with Barbara Marx Hubbard appears in chapters two and three of this book. To subscribe to Jan's newsletter, go to: www.janphillips.com.

Energizing Social Synergy for the Shift

By Claudia Welss

In a worldview that describes the universe as both holographic and holonic—that is, innately coherent, with the whole reflected in each part and each whole a part of a greater whole—we can sense the profound significance of Barbara Marx Hubbard's image of ourselves as the "universe in person," and all that implies.

In our Anthropocene age, human behavior is rightly acknowledged as a driving force in the evolution—or devolution—of Earth's natural and social systems. The new term "evomimicry" describes our efforts to learn and emulate cosmic principles to support conscious evolution. We know, for example, that coherence and synergy are at play in the universe, creating the conditions for "radical newness" to emerge in physical and biological systems; but how do we embody these principles for the same effect in social systems? And how does this relate to Barbara's claim that "the inner shift and the outer shift are the same"?

In *The Powers of the Universe*, cosmologist Brian Swimme states, "Life has a new demand on us—the demand of synergy through conscious self-awareness." Our hypothesis, based on my research at the nexus of heart coherence and social synergy, is that the "demand of synergy" can be met through an attention to heart coherence—and that the resulting state of "inner synergy" is a necessary condition for the successful expression of "outer synergy" in social systems.

The practice of heart coherence enables inner synergy by creating the physiological conditions for its emergence. It allows us to *embody synergy,* and in so doing, to become architects of global change by cocreating the energetic field conditions under which social synergy is more likely to emerge. In other words, in the Hub of the Wheel, as Barbara calls it, we use our own heart resonance to imprint the invisible field of energy that connects all things with greater resonance.

Defining Heart Coherence

Heart coherence as it is defined by the Institute of HeartMath is a state of optimal human well-being and performance, driven by the heart, in which the various systems of the body (such as the cardiovascular, endocrine, respiratory, and nervous systems) are synchronized, communicating fully, and attuned to one another. Our degree of heart coherence varies with the degree of order, stability, and harmony in the various rhythmic activities of the body's systems over time. As such, it is the body's "resonant frequency."

Heart coherence is a *measurable* psychophysiological state. Biofeedback measurements allow us to recognize it in the sine waveform patterns that result from the ordered beat-to-beat changes in the heart's rhythms (called "heart rate variability"), which in turn result from feelings of love, gratitude, compassion—or any sustained, authentic positive emotion. HeartMath refers to this coherent waveform as "the physiological signature of love at the core of the human system." By contrast, incoherence is a state characterized by lack of synchronization and disharmony, and exhibits an absence of order in heart rate variability recognizable by its erratic pattern.

HeartMath has demonstrated that we can intentionally change our heart signal pattern to a coherent waveform by feeling and working with positive emotions, a finding published by the *American Journal of*

Cardiology. Beyond being a mere pump, the heart is continually signaling the entire body. When the heart is in coherence, this state generates the signal for initiating and sustaining system-wide coherence.

The heart's signals are affected by its own intrinsic nervous system, a bundle of neurons that qualifies as its own brain; this brain in the heart communicates to the brain in our heads—in fact, more information travels from the heart to the head than vice-versa. In response to positive emotion, the heart's rhythms begin to shift to a more coherent pattern from an incoherent pattern that reflects stress.

Thus, when the heart's signal is coherent, all other bodily systems begin to resonate with that coherent pattern. Heart-brain alignment is created, causing a favorable cascade of neural, hormonal, and biochemical changes as systems synchronize and connect, facilitating system-wide communication. Among the many positive changes: the two parts of the autonomic nervous system that function like the gas and brake pedals of a car start to synchronize instead of working against each other.

Cellular biologist Bruce Lipton has said that intelligence *emerges* when a system connects with itself. In the same way, the harmonious flow of information, cooperation, and order among the body's individual systems allows for the emergence of more complex functions, such as creativity. In other words, coherence is a state of connected intelligence in which the subsystems of the body are in communication with each other, allowing for a natural inner synergy to emerge in which each individual system is mutually enhancing, producing a more intelligent, whole human system than the sum of its individual parts imply. Systems biologist Peter Corning calls this kind of synergy "nature's magic." By increasing heart coherence we are consciously aligning with the forces of "nature's magic" to extend its benefits to the physical, biological, and social realms.

Coherence as nature's pattern of connected intelligence is our birthright, but the proper conditions must be present to reclaim it. In this period of accelerated change, when systems are far from states of equilibrium, we can experience a form of incoherence called "future shock," a term Alvin Toffler coined that refers to the stress, disorientation, and disconnection people experience when exposed to too much change in too short a time. Much of the world believes our nervous systems haven't had sufficient time to adapt to the bombardment of daily stressors. In fact, it's perfectly normal to experience incoherence while simply engaging in normal daily activities. But chronic states of stress, such as fear, frustration, and anxiety can further agitate the nervous system and increase incoherence in the whole human system, affecting us not only at the cellular level but also permeating our ecosystem of self, other, and world. Recognizing and seizing moment-to-moment opportunities to shift into greater heart coherence, thereby increasing our personal coherence *baselines*, becomes one of our most essential "gifts to the Shift."

Scaling Heart Coherence for Social Synergy

The effects of heart coherence—as well as of incoherence—are not limited to the body that's expressing them. The body's systems generate numerous fields of energy at various frequencies that radiate outwards from the body as wave fields in all directions. The heart's electromagnetic field, the strongest electrical field of the body, conveys our patterns of coherence into our environment. This field can be detected several feet from the body with sensitive magnetometers, and suggests to us that a mechanism exists for the scaling of coherence. Research at HeartMath has confirmed that a person's coherent electromagnetic signals can be detected in the nervous systems of other people as well as in animals. Heart coherence thus appears to enliven our connections through resonance, not only with each other and with nature but, conceivably, with the mind of the cosmos, enabling the parts to be in communication with the whole. Perhaps this is why the Upanishads call the heart "the fulcrum of the cosmos."

The Global Coherence Initiative, a project of Heart-Math, is based on the belief that coherence *scales*—from the personal, to the social, to the planetary—and that we're always either contributing to "global stress waves" (collective incoherence) or "global coherence waves" (collective coherence). In other words, because we can intentionally change our heart signals, we can choose to take responsibility for which "standing wave" we support. This choice becomes even more important because of increasing agreement in the scientific community that the magnetic fields of the sun and the earth affect our lives in numerous ways, and that we are now at the beginning of a new cycle of solar activity that can create tremendous energetic influxes in Earth's fields. These influxes can create very dynamic conditions, and our personal levels of coherence may be a key factor in helping humanity make the most of them.

If heart coherence does indeed scale, our attempts at social synergy would benefit on all levels. At the individual level, for example, coherence creates "cortical facilitation," during which the areas of the brain responsible for higher-order functioning engage, leading to increased mental clarity, creativity, broadened perception, and greater access to intuition, increasing our general effectiveness. (Incoherence leads to "cortical inhibition," which is exactly what it sounds like.) At the social level, heart coherence creates a resonant field for the flow of information, and due to increased heart-brain alignment, communications within groups become more authentic, leading to increased social cohesion. Coherence also has several *planetary* field environment properties useful to the emergence of synergy in social systems:

1) Coherent energy moves together and persists, while incoherent energy cancels itself out. Consider the difference between laser light, which is spatially coherent and capable of burning a hole through steel (and is precise enough for micro-surgery), and incandescent light, which is spatially incoherent and can't do either of these things. Buckminster Fuller described synergy as synthesis plus energy; it should follow that synthesis plus *coherent* energy yields a more powerful form of synergy.

2) Coherent energy moves with minimum dissipation, meaning it generates minimum entropy. Entropy is the loss of information, or order, in a system. Coherence promotes negentropy, the *gaining* of information in a system, fostering more complex order and benefitting a system's positive evolution.

3) In a coherent system, the part has full access to the intelligence of the whole at the same time the part experiences maximum freedom, promoting a behavior that evolutionary biologist Elisabet Sahtouris calls "negotiated self-interest." By creating the conditions that allow for maximizing the good of the part within the context of what's good for the whole, coherence appears to be the pattern intelligence of nature promoting the greatest extent of connectivity and freedom, enabling nature to take jumps through greater synergy.

Incoherence creates separation and obstructs communication at all levels. When information exchange is constrained, a system can fall into disequilibrium. We can predict the influence of human incoherence and the resulting disequilibrium on the social systems arising from such conditions. Attention to the *energetic design* underlying our attempts at synergy seems as important, then, as attention to the *social design*. In fact, the success of the social architecture seems reliant on the quality of the energetic architecture from which it arises. The Hub, the Wheel of Cocreation, Shift Circles, and Syncons are all social design innovations intended to help us "jump the gap." But we also need to consciously design environments capable of supporting them. Without our conscious attention, it is our unconscious that informs this field by default. While the *capacity* for expressing coherence is innate, conscious proficiency in setting this capacity in motion is an inner technology that satisfies the Hub function of creating a coherent field that enables synergistic convergence.

A New Social Function

In fulfilling the new Hub social function of scaling heart coherence, we commit to helping create the conditions for the emergence of greater synergy in the world through attention to our own inner states, reflecting the truth in the saying, "the world is as we are." We act on our ability to be causal by in-forming the field with our own coherence—from wherever we are, in whatever we're doing, whenever we can—trusting we're part of a growing global community doing the same. We proceed with the confidence that through heart coherence, we repattern ourselves for inner synergy, which helps guide synergy in our lives and our world toward a repatterning of the whole in harmony with nature's intelligence. We sense that, regardless of external improvements in organizational structures, social processes, collaboration technologies, etc., any positive redesign of our world will not hold until our internal patterns change. The inner shift and the outer shift are the same.

During an interview for a recent Agents of Conscious Evolution teleseminar, philosopher Ken Wilber said he believes certain patterns of invisible form will accompany the emergence of Homo universalis, and added that the way humanity will know we're making the Shift is through a palpable intensification of the feeling of love. As the physiological signature of love at the core of the human system, the heart's coherent waveform is such a pattern of invisible form—one that HeartMath has demonstrated can be liberated by intentionally working with our positive emotions. Through this waveform we reclaim our cosmic inheritance and restore our innate coherence with all of life.

Certain theories of evolution (such as those of James Mark Baldwin and Jean-Baptiste Lamarck) state that sustained changes in behavior can shape the evolution of a species. As stated earlier in this book, the Global Coherence Initiative estimates that three-hundred and fifty thousand people measurably increasing their heart coherence baselines may be enough to create a "global coherence heart-field environment"—a field in which, through the sustained repetition of this new behavior by a critical mass of individuals, an effect may be produced that makes it easier for others to raise their coherence baselines. By intentionally generating this field of global coherence for the Shift, we may create the conditions for humanity to successfully meet life's "new demand of synergy through conscious self-awareness" and emerge as a positive, conscious evolutionary force.

Claudia Welss is on the board of the Foundation for Conscious Evolution developing the meme of evomimicry, a member of the extended research faculty of the Institute of Noetic Sciences, and founder of NextNow Collaboratory, an ongoing experiment in social synergy. She sits on the steering committee of the Global Coherence Initiative (GCI) and returned recently from England where she helped install the latest GCI magnetometer. Before her involvement with GCI, Claudia introduced the HeartMath concepts and technologies to global corporations as director of executive development programs at the Haas School of Business, University of California, Berkeley.

End Notes

1. A comprehensive overview of the worldview of conscious evolution is provided in *Conscious Evolution: Awakening the Power of Our Social Potential* (New World Library, 1998; new edition forthcoming in 2012). Also, the DVD, "What is Conscious Evolution?" is available at my website: www.evolve.org. (You may also view this entire video in the QR code provided in chapter 2.)

2. For more information on the Agents of Conscious Evolution online course: go to www.evolve.org or theshiftnetwork.com.

3. *Our Story* DVD is available at www.HumanityAscending.com.

4. Please consult *The Evolutionary Communion: The Sacred Way of Conscious Evolution* (Foundation for Conscious Evolution, 2011). This product is a guidebook along with a CD, and is available at www.evolve.org.

5. My sister, Patricia Ellsberg, and I have developed a powerful online course called Emergence: The Shift from Ego to Essence (see www.evolve.org). We guide you through a life-changing experience of becoming your own Essential Self by educating your "local selves"—that may feel separate, reactive, and afraid—to come into the heart of the inner Beloved. Deep communion and community is generated

through this course; of all the practices we offer, this is the most important. You may also want to consult *Emergence: The Shift from Ego to Essence* (Hampton Roads, 2011). For more information, see "Recommended Resources."

6. *52 Codes for Conscious Self Evolution: A Process of Metamorphosis to Realize Our Full Potential Self.* Foundation for Conscious Evolution, 2011. (Available at www.evolve.org.)

7. You may join with others around the globe in synchronous heart coherence sessions in the Global Care Room three times each day—or visit any time. Please see: www.globalcarerooms.org.

8. We have this special note on "coherence-builders" from Doc Childre, founder of HeartMath: "People's daily experiences affect the quality of their meditations and prayers, and the strength of their intentions fluctuate along with focus. Due to the Shift energies on the planet, these fluctuations are increasing, and even seasoned meditators know that anyone can spin out of coherence. Transmissions for increasing coherence in the planetary energetic field are about how much *actual* coherence is being added to the collective consciousness field. Potentially, around 350,000 people building a heart-coherence baseline is enough to allow for the percentage fluctuating in and out of coherence, and yet still achieve the baseline needed... The Global Coherence Initiative hypothesis is that: Increased *individual coherence* leads to increased *social coherence* which leads to increased *global coherence* (in the planetary energetic field environment). As people commit to increasing their personal heart-coherence baseline and radiate coherent intentions into the global field environment, it generates

a synergistic feedback loop between humanity and the earth's energetic fields. This alignment helps to raise the vibration of consciousness, which inspires a deeper heart-felt connection among each other along with increased heart-based cooperation, yielding creative solutions for taking care of the earth and all its inhabitants. (The benefits are endless, yet this is not the space to elaborate.) The goal is to realize that we are one Earth, one yard, and one people.

"Global coherence doesn't mean that every soul on the planet has to be heart coherent all at the same time. The global heart coherence baseline will increase in ratios, over time, based on individual participation and actualization. However, collective heart-based events and intentions throughout 2012, involving myriad care-agents from all parts of the world, can cause a considerable jump in the heart coherence baseline, more so than we've experienced as of yet. This increased vibration in the field environment will encourage more people than ever to pursue becoming "who they truly are" (their real self), and to take the necessary steps to actualize it. We are individually responsible for sorting out "what's our old self" and "what's the new," then using our heart's intuitive guidance to help make the needed upgrade and align with our authentic nature. As we individually change, so does the planetary well-being."

For more on cultivating heart coherence, visit www.HeartMath.com.

9. Anderson, Carolyn, with Katharine Roske, *The Co-Creators Handbook: An Experiential Guide for Discovering Your Life's Purpose and Building a Co-creative Society* (Global Family, 2001).

10. For more information on The Vistar Foundation, see "Recommended Resources."

11. Marian Head, *Suprasexual rEvolution: A Radical Path to 2012 and Beyond* (Marlin Press, 2009).

12. *The Evolutionary Communion*, op. cit.

13. *Conscious Evolution*, op. cit.

14. *Visions of a Universal Humanity*, DVD, can be found at: www.visionsthemovie.com.